CREATIVE ESCAPES

Adventures in Writing for Grades 7–12

BARBARA CHRISTIAN

FEARON TEACHER AIDS

a division of

David S. Lake Publishers

Belmont, California

ISBN–0–8224–1631–X

Library of Congress Catalog Card Number: 80–65477

Printed in the United States of America.

1 9 8 7 6

CONTENTS

CHAPTER 4 Run Away with Words

37

CHAPTER 5 Cruise to Clarity

55

CHAPTER 6 Explore Points of View

69

CHAPTER 7   Soar with Description

91

CHAPTER 8   Take Off on the Greats

105

INTRODUCTION

Creative Escapes is a source of ideas for teachers of English and creative writing in the middle and secondary grades. It contains numerous activities that not only emphasize selective skills and concepts required by the curriculum, but incorporate them in very original and innovative formats designed to free the creative energies of students fettered by ordinary classroom learning. For both teachers and students, these activities are a welcome escape from the tedious drills and tired topics featured in most grammar and composition texts.

    Creative Escapes is in part written with the current national demand for gifted/talented programs in mind. Recognizing that the needs of exceptionally bright students mainstreamed in the classroom are as difficult to meet as those of slow or nonmotivated students, it offers activities applicable on several levels. Specially designed to have a general appeal to both junior and senior high students, each activity provides step-by-step directions for students who are satisfied to follow patterns and structure in practicing a skill. However, each activity also has built-in, flexible outlets for the creative escape of students who are chafed by prescribed activities or bored by the common goal, and who may find greater challenge and satisfaction in taking the assignment a step beyond what is required of them. This flexibility takes shape in options and variations which open the way to greater growth in the one area of study and/or parallel growth in another.

    The flexible design of *Creative Escapes* also helps an instructor tailor activities to individual classes. It is unlikely that any two English classes, as a group, will have the same social or academic personality. An instructor may wish to use variations on the basic activity to approach the same skill with different groups, thereby providing individualized instruction with a minimum of additional preparation time.

Motivation

    The success of the activities included in *Creative Escapes* rests in part in their appeal to the concerns and needs of the young adult. Students don't think exclusively about English in English class; they are preoccupied with self-identity, social interaction, music, media, and other interests which entertain their thoughts outside the classroom. These preoccupations are utilized for their motivational value in many of the activities. For example, Starship Radio Message examines what we reveal of ourselves in our writing and speech and exploits interest in popular science fiction; the Communication Game points out the very real, human need for logical communication, even among peers; Mood Music deals with the effects of media and word choice.

Besides drawing upon school life and the media, these and other activities incorporate the audiovisual and personnel resources of a school and encourage students to relate their non-literary skills and experiences to their language and expression. Images, for example, stresses the written representation of ideas and forms, but also encourages students to recognize ideas and forms translated through such mediums as mime, dance, sound recording, textile work, auto design, and architecture. Activities such as Ballad of History, Open Endings, and Role Letters reinforce material learned in other classes.

Whenever possible, brainstorming, small group work, and games are included in the activities since all three contribute to a comfortable and stimulating classroom atmosphere. Brainstorming, both on the individual and group level, is a nondiscriminatory activity that deems all related input and ideas worthy of consideration. Small groups also encourage a better sharing of ideas because they remove the pressure of simultaneous performance before the teacher and the entire class. Games muster up total classroom participation and permit students to assume leadership roles.

Such deviations from normal drills or seatwork spark both student and teacher interest and liven up daily work. Entertainment, however, is not an objective as much as a valuable by-product of *Creative Escapes*. The real objective is to provide activities broad enough to enable every student to increase skills that are already part of an established program.

Format

Creative Escapes features a chapter of activities for each of eight areas of instruction in grammar and composition. The skills focus of each activity is noted parenthetically in the table of contents for convenient reference. A teacher need only decide what aspect of grammar or composition requires attention to find an appropriate activity. In some cases, appropriate activities may be found in more than one chapter since the activities are categorized according to their *greatest* emphasis.

Each activity begins with a descriptive overview followed by a statement of its objectives and a list of materials that must be prepared or assembled beforehand. A step-by-step teaching sequence provides clear directions for managing an activity. A teaching notes section offers general comments about the activity and hints to ward off potential errors in execution. Teaching aids in the form of charts, lists, bibliographic sources, and sample texts are included wherever appropriate and convenient. Suggested variations and follow-ups come at the end of each activity and provide the teacher with further possibilities and alternative versions for that activity.

Application

No activity in *Creative Escapes* is intended to be prescriptive; all permit the teacher, as well as the student, to be creative. What each plan does provide is a classroom-proven method, possible variations, and teaching notes to warn against common pitfalls.

Without question, brainstorming, incorporating nonliterary skills, using audiovisual equipment, and forming small groups all have an inherent potential for disaster. To avoid disasters, complete preparation and participation by the instructor is essential. Group brainstorming, for instance, must be monitored to keep the ideas on target and the class behavior mannerly. It must be followed by the casting out of poor and mediocre ideas, a process that precipitates some very worthwhile evaluative discussions but requires perseverance and tact. Similarly, encouraging students to exercise their outside skills and interests can become an end in itself and undermine an English program. The teacher must constantly insist that a tangential excursion by a student be related to the classroom goal, or the student will go on energetically and thoughtlessly, forgetting the original objective of the activity. Losing sight of the goal becomes especially easy when audiovisual equipment is utilized; too often the camera, movie, or tape recording provides only a "day off" from the real focus and labors of the classroom.

Forming successful small groups is perhaps the most crucial preparation in implementing many of the lessons. So much depends upon the actual composition of the class that only brief guidelines may be given here. Group activities succeed better after a class has settled in a while because the students are then more familiar with each other, and the teacher has had time to balance abilities, interpersonal relationships, and objectives in determining the makeup of the groups. Students of similar ability are best placed together when the free flow of ideas is the main goal. When peer instruction is to play a part, a mixture of abilities works better. Compatibility, of course, must be considered at all times.

Preparation of the lesson also includes adjusting the plan to the age and maturity of the group. With teacher ingenuity and the suggested variations accompanying the lessons, the activities in *Creative Escapes* can be tailored to fit most junior and senior high English classes. Where exercises are too advanced, they may be modified or used as alternative development for advanced students. For instance, while seventh graders may not be able to imitate the grammatical styles of noted authors in Comparative and Imative Writing, they may still benefit from exposure to the comparison of such styles, and gifted individuals among them may try imitations as an alternate assignment the next time the class writes. Likewise, older students may be challenged by the relatively simple Cross-Country Race if the questions with which they are presented are precise and demanding. Ultimately, with these and the other activities contained in *Creative Escapes*, it is up to the instructor to evaluate learning levels and areas of strength and weakness in order to tailor the activities accordingly.

CHAPTER 1 Get Away with Grammar Games

1 Diagraming Game

In the Diagraming Game, class teams take turns placing parts of a sentence in their proper positions in a diagram on the board. Once a team places an element in the diagram, the opposing team may challenge the placement. Therefore, every move involves the consideration of both teams. As more demanding sentences are encountered, worthwhile discussions of grammatical structure arise.

Objectives

- Students review grammar.
- Students learn from one another in a group activity.
- Students experience visual reinforcement of previously learned grammar skills.

Materials

- sentences of varying complexity selected from a grammar text
- a stopwatch or a clock with a second hand

Teaching Sequence

1. Divide the class into two teams of mixed ability. Direct each team to select a speaker to execute their moves and voice their challenges.
2. Write one of the easier sentences on the board and draw the basic subject/verb diagram below it: _____|_____.
3. Tell the teams to take turns, word by word, working all the words of the sentence into the diagram—first conferring among themselves and then letting the speaker make the placement. When a team places a word correctly, it receives a point. Any placement is open to challenge from the other team. If a challenge is valid, the challenging team receives the point instead of the placing team.

4. Continue the game until a set of five sentences has been played and then total the scores. Let the teams choose new speakers before starting a new, more difficult set of sentences.
5. Continue the process as long as time and interest permit. Keep a record of the winning team for each set so that you can determine the grand champions at the end of the review.

Teaching Notes

• Encourage the entire class to participate in the placements and challenges. Don't leave the action up to a vocal few.
• To make the game move more quickly and to prevent teams from stalling for time, assign a time limit of 10 or 15 seconds for each placement or challenge.

Variations

a. To assure individual participation, change the rules so that each member of a team must take a turn placing a word. Monitor the activity closely, directing the more capable students toward the more difficult placements and leaving the simpler elements for the others.
b. This variation increases competition and encourages strategy. Change the rules so that only the challenging team earns points: the placing team diagrams a word and the challenging team agrees or disagrees, receiving a point only if it judges correctly. The placing team may try to mislead its challenger by deliberately misplacing the more difficult parts of speech, such as present participles and gerunds, on the diagram.
c. If a class is extremely large, more than two teams may be formed. Follow the original plan and allow *any* of the opposing teams to challenge a placement. The one that indicates disagreement first has first chance at stealing the placing team's point. If the first challenge is wrong, the other teams may challenge in turn, in the order of their voiced disagreements.
d. If class members are especially interested and are capable of self-direction, they may conduct two games simultaneously on separate blackboards. This method is more difficult for the teacher to monitor, especially when the sentences become difficult and explanations are necessary.

2 Parts of Speech
Personification

In this grammar game, students organize themselves as the individual words, phrases, and punctuation marks of a long, grammatical sentence. The goal is to include all the students in the class in the sentence. The activity provides a respite from seatwork and permits creative students to make complex contributions without confusing the rest of the class.

Objectives

- Students create a visualization of grammar at work.
- Students challenge themselves to use the most difficult grammatical constructions they have previously learned.
- Students participate at their own levels, learning from, or assisting, other students.

Materials

- grammar texts for reference

Teaching Sequence

1. Explain the game to the students. Pass out the grammar texts so that every student has a reference when questions arise during the game.

2. Select two individuals from the class and direct one to choose a one-word subject and the other to choose a one-word verb which he or she would like to represent. Once this subject/verb pair has been established, let the subject representative and the verb representative take turns assigning other class members the roles of additional words, phrases, or punctuation marks in their sentence. Encourage them to include all the helpers, tense indicators, negatives, phrases, connectors, verbals, and punctuation they have covered in their grammar studies. Insist that they incorporate all the members of the class. Advise them that individual students may stand for entire units, such as prepositional phrases.

3. Give the students large pieces of paper as they take their

places in the sentence and tell them to write down the words or marks they represent. Have them hold the papers in front of themselves so that the sentence may be "proofread" whenever necessary.

4. Stop for explanations whenever a grammar rule is violated but try to move the game quickly so that as many students as possible have an opportunity to be the subject or verb.

Teaching Notes

• If the game is bogged down by coyness or posturing on the part of the subject/verb pair, challenge them to complete their sentence with a time limit, with only a few time-outs allowed for the explanation of errors. If the time limit or time-outs are exceeded, dissolve the sentence and choose a new subject/verb pair.

• The students should be reminded to include all the sentence elements they have studied.

• If the subject/verb pair runs out of ideas before the class or the time is used up, allow other class members to suggest additions for the remainder of that game.

Variations

a. To decrease the pressure and attention on the subject/verb pair, let class members join the sentence on their own initiative once the central pair is chosen. In this approach, each student must create a part for him- or herself in each game, so that everyone feels a greater personal involvement.

b. Make the game team competitive by dividing the class into two heterogeneous groups which do the same exercise simultaneously. The first group to include all its members in a grammatically correct sentence wins. The original version and variations *a* and *c* will work in a competitive framework.

c. Instead of calling upon the students to supply the sentences, come to class with the various parts of prepared sentences already transcribed on large pieces of paper. Each piece of paper should have written on it a single word, phrase, or punctuation mark. Hand out the dismembered sentences one at a time and let the students rebuild them by themselves. Intervene just enough to keep an orderly, logical approach to the activity.

③ Cross-Country Race

The Cross-Country Race is a competitive review game in which individual students answer questions in order to advance their teams on the race trail. It is easily complicated or simplified for varying age and ability levels, and it may be adapted to sports other than cross-country running. The amount of chance and surprise built into the game may also be manipulated by the teacher.

Objectives

- Students participate individually in a grammar review game.
- Students learn from one another in a team setting.

Materials

- list of review questions based on grammar rules
- a race trail drawn on a chalkboard or posted on a bulletin board (see Teaching Aid No. 1)
- colored pieces of chalk or tacks to be used as markers for the teams
- a pair of dice, one die for each team (you may substitute spinners numbered to six or sets of draw cards numbered to six)

Teaching Sequence

1. Draw or post the trail before class.
2. Divide the class into heterogeneous groups and explain the following rules of the game:
   a. The teacher has a set of review questions which will be used consecutively during the race. The teams proceed from start to finish as their members answer questions and advance according to the number thrown on a die (or spun on a wheel or turned up on a card).
   b. Each person on each team will take a turn trying to advance the team's marker on the trail. The person answers a review question and then throws a number on the die. If the question is answered correctly, the team may advance the number of spaces indicated on the die. If the

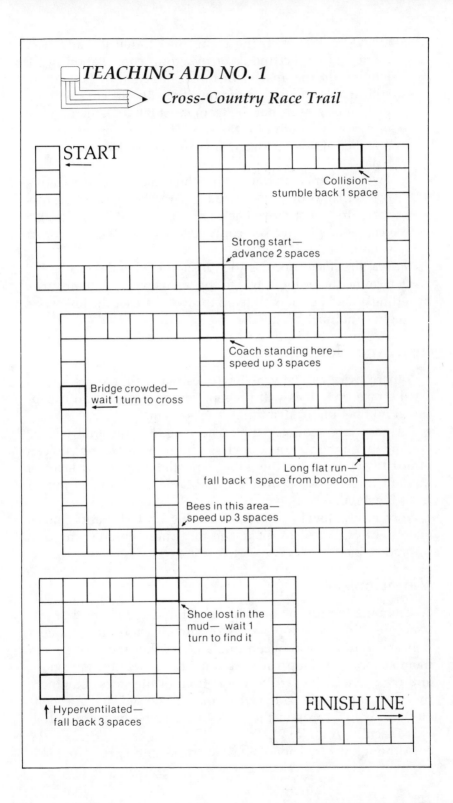

answer is incorrect, the team must forfeit the advancement and correct the error by group consultation or by looking up the answer in the grammar text. If they are still unable to answer the question, the teacher will explain the answer, but the team must fall back the number of spaces indicated on the die. The game proceeds as a member of the next team answers a question and throws a die.

c. Two markers may not occupy the same space. If a team's marker lands on an occupied square, the marker that was there first must move back a square. If that square is also occupied, the marker continues back to the first open square.

d. The first team to cross the finish line wins the race.

3. Determine the order in which the teams will take their turns by letting a member of each team throw for either the lowest or the highest number on the die.

Teaching Notes

• Prepare twice as many review questions as there are spaces on the race trail. This will prevent running short if an exceptional number of errors and fall-backs occur.

• Design a cross-country trail. The length of the trail will be contingent on the size of your class, the amount of time you can afford to set aside for the game, and the anticipated level of student interest. Keep in mind that large classes need longer trails if everyone is to get a turn.

• Work a few novelty squares featuring obstacles and chance events into the trail to make the race more entertaining and unpredictable.

Variations

a. Combine the review question sheet and the method of advancement by preparing a stack of cards, each bearing a question and a number between one and six. Let the active team member draw the top card, attempt to answer the question, and then return the card to the bottom of the stack. Laminate the cards if possible so that they may be reused. Include penalty and bonus cards in the pack to intensify the game action (see Teaching Aid No. 2).

b. Although the trail adapts best to cross-country running, ski-

TEACHING AID NO. 2

Sample Bonus
and Penalty Cards
(optional if numbered cards are used)

LEAD RUNNER STUMBLES.
Answer this question and advance to the space ahead of the lead team's marker: (question)

COMPETITION GETS TALKATIVE.
Ask the team that draws next to answer this question for you: (question)

TEAM RUNS AS A PACK.
You have the option of conferring with your teammates on this question: (question)

ENERGY SPURT.
Advance three spaces, no questions asked.

SHOE COMES UNTIED.
Answer this question and fall back to the space behind the last team's marker: (question) If you answer incorrectly and your team is unable to provide the correct answer, fall back the additional number of spaces indicated on the die.

RUNNING ORDER CHANGES.
Answer this question and send the team of your choice back two spaces: (question)

ing, swimming, or track, it can be converted to a basketball, football, or baseball game. Eliminate the trail and just use the numbers thrown or chosen to build up a team score. Rewrite the bonus and penalties to imitate the rewards and hazards of the chosen sport.

c. Duplicate the materials so that the race may be run in small groups. Give each group a trail, some markers, and either a question sheet and die or a stack of question cards. Provide an answer sheet or put the answers on the cards so that the students may correct themselves. Observe and help where needed.

4 Error Hunt

Many students' reading is limited to catchy advertisements and simply written articles in magazines. As you would expect, their writing styles reflect what they read. In the Error Hunt, students analyze a variety of ads and learn to distinguish between the elliptical style of advertising copywriters and formal prose. Having established some criteria, they apply them next to various magazine articles to determine which are well written. Finally, they rewrite fragmented ads so they contain only full sentences.

Objectives

- Students learn to recognize popular grammatical errors, especially sentence fragmentation.
- Students establish criteria for prose that is well written.
- Students practice writing complete, fluid sentences.

Materials

- ads and excerpted articles of varying literary merit, clipped from magazines that are popular with students
- an opaque projector

Teaching Sequence

1. Display several ads on the board with an opaque projector. As a group, pick out the slang phrases, slogans, and fragmented writing characteristic of some of the advertising. Consider how the style of an ad reflects the opinion the copywriter has of a reader's maturity, intelligence, reading ability, and sophistication.
2. Discuss as a group what reasons a copywriter may have for writing in an oversimplified manner. Stress that advertisements are intended to make an effective sales pitch and that the conversational style is not to be imitated in formal writing. Compare the well-written ads to the fragmented ones, pointing out the flow and balance of the one and the blunt and choppy style of the other.
3. Hand out the copies of the excerpts from magazine articles.

Ask students to apply their criteria to these longer pieces of prose. Compare the length of the sentences, the freshness of expression, and the vocabulary used in the articles. Describe the age, education, and maturity of the intended audience for each. Point out the superiority of fully developed sentences for communicating ideas at length and suggest that the students strive for the more mature style in their own writing.

4. Discuss the ways to eliminate fragmentation. For homework, assign each student a fragmented ad or article to rewrite in complete, fluid sentences.

Teaching Notes

• Insulting the students' tastes will not change their reading habits and will decrease their willingness to read the ads and excerpts critically. Be tactful. Establish the characteristics of good writing and let the students themselves compare the articles for adherence to those qualities. Be sure the students realize that what is acceptable in advertising may not be acceptable in formal prose. The object is to discourage your students' inclinations to imitate ad style.

• Ask an elementary teacher or reading specialist to help you establish the reading level of the ads and articles you have selected. Have this information at hand during the discussions in steps 2 and 3.

• Grade the rewrites for successful adherence to the criteria established in step 3.

Variations

a. With more capable groups, hand out the ads in step 1, instead of using the opaque projector. Let the students pick out the slang, slogans, and fragments by themselves and individually present their findings to the class.

b. Combine the Error Hunt with activity 15, Hard Sell Commercial. Discuss how readers are manipulated by presentation.

c. For an imitative writing assignment, require each student to write two ads or articles, one in a simple and fragmented style, and the other in a more sophisticated manner.

CHAPTER 2 Safari into Structural Grammar

5 Sentence Formulas

Approaching grammar through an alternative method both freshens the subject and provides an additional handle by which students may grasp it. Sentence Formulas is an alternative which stresses grammatical logic by treating sentences like mathematical equations. It is a valuable reinforcement and review mechanism to use throughout the regular grammar program. It has a built-in flexibility which allows advanced students to accelerate without undue attention.

Objectives

- Students observe the logical and cumulative structure of grammar.
- Students rely upon reason rather than upon possibly erroneous habits to solve grammar problems.
- Students advance to more interesting and challenging formulas at their own individual rates.

Materials

- formula exercises which vary in complexity and style (see Teaching Aid No. 3)

Teaching Sequence

1. Combine the formula method with the textbook method from the very beginning of grammar studies. Start with the simple equation: subject + verb = sentence. Ask the students to write their own simple subject + verb sentences. Have them also pick out the simple subject + verb equation in sentences from their textbooks.

2. As grammar studies progress, work the new grammar elements into the basic equation:

subject + verb = sentence
article + noun = subject
$\therefore$ article + noun + verb = sentence

preposition + article + noun = prepositional phrase
preposition + article + noun $\neq$ sentence

3. Monitor the progress of each student, directing more capable individuals into more challenging formulas, such as those involving verbals, clauses, and other parts of speech which constitute the formation of compound-complex sentences.

TEACHING AID NO. 3

Sample Sentence
Formula Exercises

1. Match set sentences to set formulas.
   a. The cat under the bed will not purr.
   b. Some people who are friends fight quite often.
   c. In the night the burglar stole the jewels.

   1. article + noun + preposition + article + noun + future helper verb + adverb + verb (a)
   2. preposition + article + noun + article + noun + past tense verb + article + noun (c)
   3. indefinite adjective + noun + relative pronoun + linking verb + predicate noun + verb + adverb + adverb (b)

2. Write the formula to fit a set sentence.
   a. Mary, who was a new girl, had no friends.
   a. proper noun + relative pronoun + past tense linking verb + article + adjective + noun + past tense verb + adjective + noun.
   b. Perhaps you will travel next summer.

   b. adverb + personal pronoun + future helper verb + verb + adjective + noun

3. Write a sentence to fit a set formula.
   a. article + noun + prepositional phrase + linking verb + adverb + adjective
   a. The trout in the frying pan is very uncomfortable.

   b. Infinitive clause + linking verb + possessive pronoun + noun + conjunction + personal pronoun + future helper verb + adverb + verb + particle
   b. To do the job correctly is my goal, and I shall never give up.

Teaching Notes

• Students accept the method more quickly if it is used persistently from the very beginning of grammar studies. Problems based upon the formulas should appear on the regular grammar tests, even if only as alternate questions.

• In the exercises, filling in random words of a certain part of speech is challenging. Some students may initially need reference lists of words organized by part of speech in order to complete the formulas.

• The formula exercises used should be varied in style just as math problems are. (see Teaching Aid No. 3). Be certain that answers can't be determined by such an easy means as counting words.

• The formulas should be graded the same as any other grammar assignments.

Variation

Punctuation may be included in the formulas. End marks may be added merely with a + sign, for example, and commas may be inserted with a + sign on either side and parenthetical comments about the reasons they are used:

 a. The rain, sleet, and snow created disastrous driving conditions.
 a. article + noun + comma (series) + noun + comma (series) + conjunction + noun + past tense verb + adjective + present participle + noun + period (end of sentence)
 b. She met with the judge, and the judge heard her case.
 b. personal pronoun + past tense verb + preposition + article + noun + comma (compound sentence) + conjunction + article + noun + past tense verb + possessive pronoun + noun + period (end of sentence)

⑥ Comparative Grammars

Language students often comment that they understand their own language better after studying another because working in an unfamiliar vocabulary forces them to use the elements of grammar as tools. Comparative Grammars takes advantage of this insight with a foreign language activity which demonstrates the functional nature of grammar. Students learn the value and logic of grammar rules as they translate simple sentences from one language to another.

Objectives

- Students learn that grammar is a universal among languages because it organizes the relationships language is meant to convey.
- Students gain insights into the structure of their own language in the process of translating it into another.

Materials

- comparative grammar sheets (see Teaching Aid No. 4)

Teaching Sequence

1. Arrange for a foreign language speaker or teacher to spend a class period with the students. Prior to the lesson, consult with the guest speaker and draw up a comparison sheet which contains only the amount of material that can be covered in the time allotted for the exercise. Select a simple vocabulary and establish the grammar rules the students will need to learn.

2. Prepare the class ahead of time by discussing why structural grammar is a universal feature of all languages.

3. The day before the guest speaker is to come, preview the comparison sheets. Hand out the English sheet first and ask the students to fill in the selected vocabulary. As a class, review the basic grammar rules and build some sentences using the established words and rules. Then hand out the foreign language sheet and have the students fill in the vocabulary portion, taking extra care that they spell and accent the words properly. Go over the pronunciation of the foreign words and explain that the guest instructor will help the class apply the rules of the foreign language to those words in order to build sentences identical in meaning to the ones created from the English vocabulary. Collect the worksheets and set them aside for the next day.

4. On the day of the presentation, redistribute the worksheets and instruct the students to fill in the foreign grammar rules as the guest presents them. Introduce the speaker and leave him

TEACHING AID NO. 4

Sample Grammar Sheet

Each student will need two identical sheets, one for the English grammar rules and one for the foreign grammar rules. On the sample sheet which follows, some rules of English grammar which are easily used for the basis of the comparison have been inserted for your reference. The vocabulary spaces are purposely limited because a large number of words would only complicate the lesson and obscure its comparative value. Number or rule the back of each comparison sheet to make spaces for the sentences to be generated from each grammar.

VOCABULARY

Nouns   Pronouns   Adverbs   Adjectives

Articles   Prepositions   Conjunctions   Verbs
                                               (conjugated)

RULES

Noun Phrase
article + adjective + noun

Prepositional Phrases
preposition + article + noun

Indirect Objects
have an understood preposition; follow the verb, precede the direct object; verb + indirect object + direct object

Interrogative Sentences
voice inflection; subject splits helper and verb; helper + subject + verb

Pronouns as Subjects
agree with gender of antecedent; all common nouns are neuter

Direct Objects
follow the verb and the indirect object, if there is one; verb + (indirect object) + direct object

Clauses
subordinating conjunction + subject + verb, or relative pronoun + verb

Verb Conjugation
Present: all forms of regular verbs are the same except in the third person singular

Simple past: verb adds -ed or changes form

Future: all forms of regular verbs are in the present tense but are preceded by a future helper verb (the third person singular form of the present tense is ignored)

or her to conduct the class as planned in step 1. Be on hand to help the students individually when they are asked to apply the new grammar rules to the new vocabulary.

5. The next day, conduct a brief follow-up discussion on the logic and usefulness of grammar.

Teaching Notes

• The consultation in step 1 must be as thorough and productive as possible. If you are unfamiliar with the foreign language, be certain you learn the necessary vocabulary rules so that you can assist the students.

• The guest instructor should understand that English grammar is as much a focus of the lesson as the foreign grammar, and should elicit, rather than point out, comparisons.

• A teacher who is bilingual may, of course, present this lesson without assistance. However, the students enjoy a change of pace and face, and a guest instructor provides both.

• The exercises need not be graded. Their value lies in the insights they provide into the inherent structure and functional practicality of grammar.

Variation

Instead of using a real foreign language, a class may create an entirely new language of its own, using the comparison sheet as a planner. Much may be learned through eliminating or complicating the parts of speech and grammar rules of the new language.

7 Comparative and Imitative Writing

Comparing and imitating the writing styles of recognized writers is a challenging assignment requiring thorough planning and involvement on the part of the teacher as well as conscientious work from the students. For the first part of the lesson, the students analyze and compare the grammatical structure of short excerpts from several authors' works. A lecture on elements of style provides them with the criteria to make critical observations on the stylistic differences illustrated in the excerpts. Then those students who feel they can, attempt to imitate the writing of two authors with dissimilar styles.

Only serious, advanced students should be expected to handle the entire activity, although an entire class may be capable of comparing styles that are radically different.

Objectives

- Students observe that an underlying grammatical structure is behind the distinctive styles that characterize the works of great writers.
- Students observe that writing styles may differ greatly and still have artistic merit.

Materials

- writing samples from six or eight noted authors, duplicated with room so that students may write on the copies
- a prepared lecture discussing the writing samples (see Teaching Aid No. 5)
- a worksheet applying the analytical details of the lecture to the samples (see Teaching Aid No. 5)
- marking pens of as many light colors as possible

Teaching Sequence

1. Allow the students as much time as necessary to read the writing samples you have prepared and distributed.
2. Ask the students to select representative sentences from as many samples as possible. Give them the markers and tell them to highlight various grammatical elements of each sentence: subject noun, verb, complete subject, complete predicate, prepositional phrases, subordinate clauses, adjectives, and others. This highlighting, which yields a colorful diagram of an author's structural style, may be done as a group work if a teacher or some other resource person is available for guidance.
3. As a group project, let the students arrange the authors' works in a hierarchy of grammatical complexity. This activity will help demonstrate that good literature may be written at any level of complexity and will make evident the stylistic differences among noted authors.
4. Present a lecture on the elements of style. (see Teaching Aid No. 5) Encourage a follow-up discussion.

☐ TEACHING AID NO. 5

➤ *Suggested Guidelines for the Lecture and Worksheet*

Authors John Steinbeck   J. R. R. Tolkien
             Ernest Hemingway   Stephen Crane
             Henry James   Edith Wharton
             Katherine Anne Porter William Faulkner
             F. Scott Fitzgerald LeRoi Jones

Elements of Style:

The worksheet should provide specific examples from the texts to illustrate these elements discussed in a lecture:
- the extent to which the author uses descriptive grammatical elements (adverbs, adjectives, phrases, clauses, active construction)
- the complexity of the sentences (simple, compound, complex, compound-complex), their number and mixture; an interesting ratio of simple-to-difficult can be established for each author
- the use of poetic conventions (alliteration, metaphors, imagery, rhythm)
- the overall tone of the selection (brusque, friendly, intense, austere, reportorial)
- the frequency and the type of dialogue (wordy, direct, emotional, differentiated for each speaker, tagged or untagged)
- the type of detail included (physical action, descriptive matter, emotional or mental processes, dialogue, dialogue tags, asides to the reader)
- the point of view (omniscient, limited omniscient, first person, direct observer)
- the special effects of the various styles (brisk and unemotional; sensitive and involved; intellectual and formal; private and psychological)

---

5. Pass out a worksheet which lists the elements of style covered in the lecture. Have students select two or three of the samples distributed earlier and write a one- or two-page paper about the authors' styles, using the elements of style to support their observations and comparisons.
6. Direct the capable students to individually select two

authors with radically different writing styles and to create 300 to 500 words of prose imitating each style. Remind them to mimic both the grammatical and elemental styles of their models.

7. Post the imitations alongside copies of the appropriate original excerpts.

Teaching Notes

• Selections should be typical of their authors and different from one another. Include examples of stream of consciousness writing (Faulkner), as well as some very difficult third person prose (James), and some very clear, direct writing (Hemingway).

• The intricacies of style are advanced concepts and the students should not be expected to master them with only tapes and worksheets for reference. While some students go on to write creative imitations, others may need some clarification and review. The instructor should arrange either to divide his or her time between the small group and the class, or to have a knowledgeable aide assist with the class during the divergent activities.

• Grade the highlighting exercise, the worksheet, and the imitative writing separately. Grades should be based upon an understanding and application of the principles of grammatical structure and elements of style covered in the activity.

Variation

Remove the names from the creative imitations and duplicate them to use as the basis for a follow-up discussion. As a group, read each imitation and try to identify its model. Point out the major characteristics which were mimicked.

CHAPTER 3 Wander through Reference Books

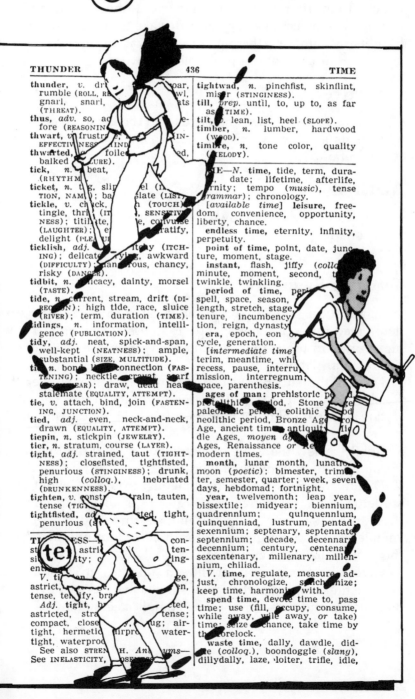

thunder, *v.* dr... oar, rumble (ROLL, RE...wl, gnarl, snarl, ...ts (THREAT).

thus, *adv.* so, ac... e-fore (REASONIN...

thwart, *v.* frustr... IN-EFFECTIVENESS...IND...

thwarted, ...a foile...d, balked (...URE).

tick, *n.* ...beat, (RHYTHM...

ticket, *n.* t...g, slip...el (...TION, NAM...); ba...late (LIST...

tickle, *v.* ch...ck, ...n (TOUCH), tingle, thri... (IT...SENSITIV..., NESS); titil...ate, ...e, convulse (LAUGHTER); e...ratify, delight (PLE...UR...

ticklish, *adj.* ...t...y (ITCHING); delicate...yi...g, awkward (DIFFICULTY); ...an...rous, chancy, risky (DANGER).

tidbit, *n.* ...icacy, dainty, morsel (TASTE).

tide, *n.* ...rrent, stream, drift (DIREC...ON); high tide, race, sluice (RIVER); term, duration (TIME).

tidings, *n.* information, intelligence (PUBLICATION).

tidy, *adj.* neat, spick-and-span, well-kept (NEATNESS); ample, substantial (SIZE, MULTITUDE).

ti... *n.* bond...connection (FASTENING); necktie, cravat, scarf (...EAR); draw, dead heat, stalemate (EQUALITY, ATTEMPT).

tie, *v.* attach, bind, join (FASTENING, JUNCTION).

tied, *adj.* even, neck-and-neck, drawn (EQUALITY, ATTEMPT).

tiepin, *n.* stickpin (JEWELRY).

tier, *n.* stratum, course (LAYER).

tight, *adj.* strained, taut (TIGHTNESS); closefisted, tightfisted, penurious (STINGINESS); drunk, high (*colloq.*), inebriated (DRUNKENNESS).

tighten, *v.* constr...rain, tauten, tense (TIG...

tightfisted, *ad...* ...ted, tight, penurious (s...

TI...NESS— con-st...astri...ten-si...ty; c...ling-en...

V. ti...on ...ge, astrict, ...n, tense, te...ify, bra...

Adj. tight, b...cted, astricted, stra...tense; compact, close...y, ug; air-tight, hermetic...irpro...water-tight, waterproo...

See also STRE...H. An...yms— See INELASTICITY, ...OSE...

tightwad, *n.* pinchfist, skinflint, miser (STINGINESS).

till, *prep.* until, to, up to, as far as (TIME).

tilt, *v.* lean, list, heel (SLOPE).

timber, *n.* lumber, hardwood (WOOD).

timbre, *n.* tone color, quality (MELODY).

TI...E—*N.* time, tide, term, dura-...date; lifetime, afterlife, ...rnity; tempo (*music*), tense ...rammar); chronology.

[*available time*] leisure, freedom, convenience, opportunity, liberty, chance.

endless time, eternity, infinity, perpetuity.

point of time, point, date, juncture, moment, stage.

instant, flash, jiffy (*collo...* minute, moment, second, t... twinkle, twinkling.

period of time, per...d spell, space, season, ...length, stretch, stage, ...tenure, incumbency...tion, reign, dynasty...era, epoch, eon ...cycle, generation.

[*intermediate time*] ...terim, meantime, whi... recess, pause, interru...mission, interregnum; ...pace, parenthesis.

ages of man: prehistoric pe...d, pro...lithic...riod, Stone ...ge, paleol...ic per...d, eolithic ...od, neolithic period, Bronze Ag...ro... Age, ancient tim...antiqui...d... dle Ages, moyen âg...Ages, Renaissance *or* R... modern times.

month, lunar month, lunat...moon (*poetic*); bimester, trim...ter, semester, quarter; week, seven days, hebdomad; fortnight.

year, twelvemonth; leap year, bissextile; midyear; biennium, quadrennium; quinquennium, quinquenniad, lustrum, pentad; sexennium; septenary, septennate; septennium; decade, decennar... decennium; century, centena...; sexcentenary, millenary, millennium, chiliad.

V. time, regulate, measure, ad-just, chronologize, s...ch...nize; keep time, harmon...with.

spend time, devote time to, pass time; use (fill, occupy, consume, while away, wile away, *or* take) time; seize...chance, take time by th...orelock.

waste time, dally, dawdle, did-...e (*colloq.*), boondoggle (*slang*), dillydally, laze, loiter, trifle, idle,

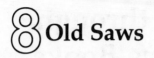# Old Saws

In this very enjoyable exercise, students may indulge their tendencies to overburden their writing with unnecessarily difficult diction. The object of the game is to take a simple saying and bury its meaning in a barrage of verbosity, using a dictionary and a thesaurus to hunt up complicated words.

Objectives

- Students improve their thesaurus and dictionary skills.
- Students see how wordiness gets in the way of clear communication.

Materials

- sample obfuscated old saws (see Teaching Aid No. 6)
- dictionaries
- thesauri

Teaching Sequence

1. Hand out a sample page of obfuscated saws. Let the students read through them silently to guess at the familiar sayings buried in the verbiage. After a few moments, ask for the simple "translations."
2. Discuss the superiority of the simple statements over the wordy ones. Define *cliché, verbiage, verbosity, obfuscation,* and *obscure meaning.* Point out how wordiness can defeat communication.
3. Briefly review the value of the dictionary and the thesaurus for finding the synonyms of words.
4. Divide the class into homogeneous groups of about four students each and give each group a dictionary and a thesaurus. Ask each group to think up three old saws to exchange with another group. After three or four minutes, have the groups make the exchange.
5. Give the groups ten or fifteen minutes to thoroughly obscure the meaning of the sayings they have received by using dictionaries and thesauri to locate complicated synonyms.

6. Ask the groups to exchange papers with a different group than before. Allow a few moments for the groups to reduce to the familiar the obfuscated saws they have received.

7. Conduct a discussion of two concepts related to the exercise: one, that finding the desirable middle ground between cliché and verbosity can freshen the restatement of an old idea; and two, that choosing synonyms merely because they are long and impressive can somewhat alter the meaning. Point out that the connotations and meanings of attractive synonyms should be checked in a dictionary before the words are used.

8. Repeat the activity if time permits.

TEACHING AID NO. 6

Sample Obfuscated Saws

1. **If at first you don't succeed, try, try again.**
When original endeavors for triumph do not achieve the immediate desirable results, never hesitate to indulge in however many necessary attempts thereafter.

2. **Red sky at night, sailor's delight.**
Atmospheres resplendent with incarnadine hue at the proximity of darkness elicit rejoicing among mariners.

3. **Every cloud has a silver lining.**
There is not in nature a mass of precipitous matter which lacks an undercoating of metallic luster.

4. **It never rains but it pours.**
Many have noted the impossibility of enjoying a gentle zephyr and precipitation; conditions always deteriorate to torrential storms.

5. **Actions speak louder than words.**
Physical accomplishments discourse at a decibel level that far surpasses the volume of verbosity.

6. **Haste makes waste.**
An excess of rapid motion often has a direct correlation to the production of utterly useless matter.

7. **Don't cry over spilt milk.**
Under no circumstances must you indulge in lamentations in the aftermath of the overrunning of the white body fluid of bovines.

Teaching Notes

• The follow-up discussion featured in step 7 is essential to the lesson and should not be eliminated to save time. Repeating the exercise after the discussion reinforces the concepts and gives the teacher a chance to encourage the back-up use of the dictionary.
• The activity incorporates two extremes of expression—the hackneyed saying and the wordy rendition. Be sure the students understand that both are to be avoided in their writing.

Variations

a. The activity can be conducted as quiet seatwork simply by rotating the papers among individuals instead of among groups. The activity is undoubtedly more enjoyable and productive as a group effort, however.
b. Have students come up with current slang expressions rather than old saws in step 4.
c. When repeating the exercise, have each group originate simple sentences instead of old saws.
d. Use the exercise in conjunction with activity 19, Burning Deadwood.

⑨ Ballad of History

The Ballad of History is a versatile writing assignment that may be combined with both poetry and history studies at all levels. The students become familiar with the distinctive characteristics of a ballad and then apply their knowledge of an historic event in a group writing effort.

Objectives

• Students learn the conventions of a literary ballad.
• Students have an opportunity to work with meter and rhyme.
• Students use the thesaurus and rhyming dictionary to expedite their search for rhythmic and rhyming words.

```
  ┌─────────────────────────────────────────────────────────┐
  │   ▭╲   TEACHING AID NO. 7                                │
  │   ▭═══╲                                                  │
  │   ▭════▷  Suggested Introductory                         │
  │           Ballads                                        │
  │                                                          │
  │   1. "Sweet Betsy from Pike" (folk song)                 │
  │   2. "Ballade of Good Counsel" (Geoffrey Chaucer)        │
  │   3. "Edward, Edward" (anonymous)—varied refrain         │
  │   4. "Sir Patrick Spens" (anonymous)—no refrain          │
  │   5. "Ballad of Birmingham" (Dudley Randall)—no refrain  │
  └─────────────────────────────────────────────────────────┘
```

Materials

- sample ballads (see Teaching Aid No. 7)
- thesauri
- rhyming dictionaries

Teaching Sequence

1. As a class, read one or two of the sample ballads. If the class is relaxed and receptive enough for group recitation, allow individuals to read the verses and let everyone join in on the refrain.

2. Examine the ballads for common elements. Record on the board the stanza length, meter, rhyme scheme, subject matter, and (if applicable) refrain.

3. Read the remaining ballads and note how they comply with the recorded conventions.

4. As a class, choose a familiar historical event. Be sure everyone knows and understands all the details and ramifications of the story. List on the board the story elements that should be included in the ballad, such as the main sequence of events, the personality and temperament of each central character, necessary background information, and the historic consequences of the event. Then choose an outstanding element and write a refrain as a class, establishing a simple meter and rhyme scheme. Use a thesaurus and a rhyming dictionary to find synonyms which fit into the meter and which spawn appropriate rhymes for other lines in the refrain.

5. Divide the class into small heterogeneous groups and assign each group an element of the story from the list on the board. Direct the groups to write one stanza in the established meter and rhyme scheme. Pass out thesauri to each group. Share the rhyming dictionaries that are available.

6. Compile and copy the results for distribution. Discuss how well each individual stanza conforms to the established pattern. As a group, make improvements where necessary. Post the final copy or submit it to the school paper.

Teaching Notes

• Save this activity for the end of a poetry unit. Although the structure of the ballad is relatively simple, working with rhyme and meter is easier if the students have had some previous experience writing poetry.

• Encourage the oral reading suggested in step 1. Ballads are an oral tradition and their characteristics are more obvious when the poems are read aloud.

• Step 4 progresses much more smoothly if the teacher prepares five or six subjects, outlines appropriate refrains for each beforehand, and then guides the discussion with these ideas in mind. The students still choose the final theme, supply the story elements, and establish a meter and rhyme scheme as a class.

Variations

a. Allow interested or musically talented students to earn extra credit by composing or arranging appropriate music for the ballad. Have them play the parts of traveling minstrels and sing the ballad to the class. Record their efforts for future classes.

b. If the general ability of the class is too low for this group project to succeed, use the Ballad of History as an alternative assignment for the more capable students while the others write individual, less structured poems on the subject. Require each student in the advanced group to write one stanza and help the group to write a refrain together.

c. Base the ballad on a current event or even on a school event. Once again, be sure all the students understand the details and ramifications of the story before the writing begins. If the results are exceptionally good, submit them to a local paper.

10) Vocabulary Story

Vocabulary Story is an innovation of an old standby activity in which students write short narratives incorporating their vocabulary or spelling words. First, students investigate the definitions of assigned vocabulary words, searching for those synonyms the closest and furthest in meaning and connotation to the original words. Next, they must brainstorm relationships between the words in the context of a coherent, if somewhat bizarre, short story narrative. After writing the story, they return to their list of synonyms, substitute first those closest, then those furthest, in meaning and connotation to the original vocabulary words used in the story. Upon rereading their stories with the substitutions, they will not fail to note balance on the one hand, and a remarkable incongruity on the other.

Objectives

- Students become sensitive to the nuances in meaning of words and their synonyms.
- Students exercise logic and imagination in order to bring a variety of words into a workable relationship.

Materials

- a vocabulary or spelling word list of 20 to 25 words
- dictionaries
- thesauri
- a vocabulary or spelling word test

Teaching Sequence

1. Hand out copies of a vocabulary list which includes the definition of each word that must be learned in preparation for a vocabulary test.
2. As a class, look up a couple of the words on the list and examine some of their additional meanings. Then look up the same words in a thesaurus to see how their meanings may be further expanded.
3. Choose one word the class has investigated and list its

meanings and synonyms on the board. As a group, arrange the synonyms in a hierarchy of meaning according to their connotations. For example, range them from positive to negative connotation, and from approximately equal in meaning with the vocabulary word to very removed in meaning. Have students complete steps 2 and 3 on their own in the same manner for every other word on the list.

4. For homework, assign a 200-word narrative incorporating 12 out of 20 (or 16 out of 25) of the vocabulary words. Stress that the story may be silly but must make sense. Remind them that the same word may often function as both a noun and a verb, and may become adverbial or adjectival with minor alterations. Allow extra credit for including more than the assigned number of vocabulary words in the story.

5. After you have approved the stories, have students refer back to the hierarchical list of synonyms they compiled in step 3. First, have them select from the list a synonym substitute that comes closest in meaning and connotation to each vocabulary word incorporated into their stories. Ask them to pencil in these words lightly above the originals and reread the stories to themselves with the substitutions. When they have finished, elicit their reactions.

6. Have them refer back again to the synonym list, but this time have them substitute those synonyms furthest in meaning and connotation from the original words used in the stories. Once they have penciled in these substitutions, invite two or three students to read aloud their original stories and these new versions. Encourage the class to comment on the striking departures in tone and obfuscation in meaning that invariably result from the changes.

7. Test the class on the vocabulary word list.

Teaching Notes

• Older or advanced students are capable of working more than the required number of vocabulary words into their stories. Challenge senior high classes to include 16 of 20 (or 20 of 25) words and encourage gifted students at all levels to incorporate as many of the words as possible.

• The spelling list should be composed of words from a manual, grammar text, or some source other than a literature or history text. The vocabulary words accompanying a story or history lesson will already be loosely related, and this established relationship will hinder creativity in the story-writing segment of the activity.

• The stories improve if students are granted the parts of speech leeway suggested in step 4. Besides simplifying the assignment, this concession encourages the students to indirectly review grammatical concepts.

• The stories should be graded on originality and on the correct usage of the vocabulary words. Look for logic and coherence but allow for minor contrivances that are necessary in order to work in the assigned words.

• Most teachers have a preferred method for testing vocabulary and spelling. One effective method is to hand out a test paper with numbered definitions typed in a column down one half of it and lettered blanks typed down the other. For the spelling portion of the test, the teacher dictates the words to be written in the blanks. For the vocabulary portion, the students record the letter of the word beside its numbered definition.

Variations

a. Junior high students may enjoy physically personifying the synonyms in the ranking process in step 3. Choose one student to represent each synonym and let the class shift the selected students around to create the hierarchy.

b. Combine this activity with the connotation and denotation activities in Chapter Four.

CHAPTER 4 Run Away with Words

11 Word Power

Readers respond to words according to their individual backgrounds and experiences, interpreting them in an immense interwoven pattern of tone and feeling (connotation) as well as by their actual definition (denotation). Creative writers rely much on connotative meanings, and objective, technical writers stress denotative ones. In this discussion and brainstorming activity, students discover the value of each approach and the differences between them.

Objectives

- Students learn the meanings of the terms *connotation* and *denotation*.
- Students observe in their class discussion the varying responses people have to a single word.

Materials

- sample dictionary definition or technical description
- sample connotation grid (see Teaching Aid No. 9)

Teaching Sequence

1. Introduce and explain the terms *connotation* and *denotation*.
2. Use a dictionary entry or a technical description (from a shop manual, for instance) to exemplify denotative meaning. Use the sample *World War II* discussion (see Teaching Aid No. 8) or a similar example to demonstrate connotative meaning.
3. To demonstrate the connotation exercise the class will do in small groups, put the word *Christmas,* or an equally emotive word, on the board. Ask for the denotative meaning and record that in a corner of the board. Then list the categories of the senses—sight, touch, sound, smell, taste, and emotion—across the board, drawing a column under each. Explain that the connotative meaning of *Christmas* exists in the sensual and emotional responses of the reader. Have class members call out their responses and list them on the board. Ask for nouns and action verbs as well as modifiers and keep listing words until at least 100 are recorded. (see Teaching Aid No. 9)

TEACHING AID NO. 8

Sample Connotation Discussion for **World War II**

1. What is brought to mind by the mention of *World War II?*

nouns: death, blood, slaughter, hunger, destruction, power, soldiers, tanks, bombs, ships, Hitler

verbs: kill, murder, burn, strafe, bomb, starve, conquer, lose

modifiers: gory, hostile, terrifying, long-drawn-out, tattered, global, suddenly, totally, deadly, immensely

2. In his *Peanuts* strip, Charles Schultz names the neighboring cat "World War II." We never see the cat, but we sense its nature and its appearance because of the connotations of its name. List some adjectives that would describe this cat: tattered, grouchy, hostile, enormous, deadly, destructive, hulking, slashing, quick, powerful.

4. Point out how using the simple, colorful proper noun *Christmas* for descriptions, as in "a Christmasy atmosphere" or "It feels like Christmas," connotes a wealth of meaning and saves both writer and reader much time and explanation.

5. Divide the class into small groups of three to five individuals. Assign each group an emotive word (see Teaching Aid No. 10) or allow the group to come up with one of its own. Let each group appoint a scribe to fill in a connotation grid on the word. Stress again the need for finding nouns and active verbs as well as modifiers and require a minimum of 50 words. Ask each group to list five additional emotive words to which the same activity could be applied.

6. Toward the end of the period, let one person from each group read the group's connotation grid. Allow the other groups to add or challenge words, discussing recommendations or comments as they are made.

Teaching Notes

• Activities such as this one which require group participation work better once a class has had time to become familiar and friendly, usually well into the school year.

TEACHING AID NO. 9

Sample Connotation Grid
for **Christmas**

Denotation: a holiday celebrated December 25 and accepted by Christians as the anniversary of Christ's birth

Connotations:

SIGHT	SOUND	TASTE
mistletoe	bells	Alka Seltzer
gifts	ho ho's	chocolate
trees	fires	turkey
holly	carols	candies
candles	organs	candy canes
wreaths	laughter	fruitcake
confections		fruit
pine cones		
tinsel		
snow		
sleigh		
lights		
trim	harmonize	stuff
go to church	shout	overeat
write cards	ring	snack
peek	chime	nip
visit	trot	sample
	jingle	savor
		devour
glittering	soothing	delicate
sparkling	exciting	tart
glowing	silvery	spicy
colorful	melodic	heady
bright	inspirational	fattening
cluttered	religious	sweet
snowy	tinny	scrumptious
frosty	nerve-wracking	
abundant		
kaleidoscopic		
twinkling		

Continued on next page.

SMELL	TOUCH	EMOTION
turkey roasting	air	cheer
pie	fire	loneliness
trees	presents	togetherness
candles	decorations	generosity
popcorn		love
cold, snowy air		brotherhood
		reflection
		depression
		faith
sniff	caress	give
savor	poke	receive
detect	wrap	kiss
revel in	tie	hope
permeate	hug	love
	buy	despair
	rip	
	kiss	
	luxuriate	
spicy	soothing	jolly
heady	prickly	festive
piney	warm	gala
heavy	frigid	generous
aromatic	fragile	fortunate
enticing		affectionate
fragrant		busy
		broke
		pressured
		lonely

TEACHING AID NO. 10

Sample Emotive Words

Halloween	spring	kindergarten
Fourth of July	summer	first day of school
New Year's Day	circus	January (or any month)

• The students will need constant reminders to use several parts of speech and to avoid lackluster description in their word hunt.

Variation

Expand the lesson to include a two-part writing assignment. Tell the students to select an item and describe it first in denotative terms, as in a definition or a technical description, and then with feeling, evincing for the reader all that the word connotes for them.

12 Positive and Negative Viewpoints

Students should learn to recognize the connotative impact of individual words and how authors make clear the feeling they wish attached to a particular word. In this exercise, students study a pair of articles revealing two very different sets of connotations for the simple word *fire*. Then they produce similar pairs of paragraphs on subject words of their own choice.

Objectives

• Students observe the personal nature of word response.
• Students tap their own responses to their own subjects in a personal writing exercise.

Materials

• copies of the two *fire* paragraphs or a similar pair of contrasting articles (see Teaching Aid No. 11)

Teaching Sequence

1. Introduce or review the terms *positive* and *negative connotation*. Discuss how one word usually carries both types of connotation, depending upon the experiences of both the reader and the writer.
2. Read the sample paragraphs about *fire*. Discuss which nouns, verbs, and modifiers create the individual tone of each paragraph. Point out the elements of contrast between them,

TEACHING AID NO. 11

Positive Connotations of Fire

With cold-stiffened fingers I opened the wood stove door and released the pent-up comfort of the fire. Warmth tumbled out and brushed against me, massaging away the goose bumps from my arms. Inside the stove the fire merrily popped a bit of spruce sap as it wrapped delicate fingers around the half-consumed logs. Swirling ghosts of perfumed smoke, the spirits of the logs, circled the chamber lazily before drifting into the chimney hole. They left behind them the faithful embers, deeply red, patterned with black crevices, comforting. Warmed and soothed, I lingered dreamily before the fire a long moment before reluctantly closing the stove door.

Negative Connotations of Fire

I burst into the room and ripped open the wood stove door, even though I knew from the breathless heat of the room and the low thunder coming from the stove that the fire was growing too great and hungry for its little box. I peered at the glaring orange and yellow flames anxiously a moment before the intensity of color and heat drove me backwards a step, and I had to turn my head sideways to catch my breath. All the air from the entire cabin seemed to be rushing past me to the stove, compelled to feed the maniacal god within it. Inside, sap sizzled out of the logs. Sparks, smoke, and flames streaked for the chimney hole with thin squeals. In the spectacle I could see a flaming house, a flaming forest. Frantically I closed the door and damper, turning nature upon nature, and begged the demon fire to die.

such as the appearance of the flames, the behavior of the smoke, the degree of heat, and the attitude of the author.

3. Choose a simple subject word like *fire*. Ask the class to brainstorm first its positive connotations and then its negative ones, recording both in columns on the board. Work each set of ideas into a paragraph outline.

4. Assign two paragraphs based on the positive and negative connotations of a subject word chosen independently by each student. Allow several days before the due date so that the

students have time to observe their subject and determine their responses. Mention the value of a thesaurus in finding the word that has exactly the right shade of meaning for an individual response.

5. Read aloud or post the more sensitive descriptions.

Teaching Notes

• Students enjoy the exercise but some have difficulty selecting subject words. Conduct a brainstorming session in class and briefly discuss the positive and negative angles of some of the suggested words.

• Steer the students away from general, lackluster descriptions such as "pretty," "big," or "ugly." Stress the use of nouns and active verbs as well as modifiers to express the desired precise meaning.

Variations

a. Expand the lesson to show the many shades of meaning every word has between the positive and negative extremes. Choose a word with a large entry in the thesaurus. As a class, discuss what is implied by each synonym or antonym, and rank these by the degree of good or bad feeling, or just by the variation of meaning from strong and expressive to weak and colorless.

b. Expand the length of the writing assignment. The approach works equally well for expanded compositions or even short stories.

13 Single Effect

Most students must be encouraged to search beyond everyday, colorless descriptive words to find the precise words for their purposes. This listening/writing assignment employs recordings of masterfully written descriptions to demonstrate the power of the appropriate word. The small group activity illustrates the common effect of specific descriptive words and provides the students with sounding boards for their ideas.

Objectives

- Students listen for descriptive words that create the overall effect of a piece of a writing.
- Students study Edgar Allan Poe's theory of "single effect."
- Students brainstorm appropriate words and, as a group, write paragraphs which create a single effect.

Materials

- recordings of highly descriptive literature (see Teaching Aid No. 12)
- thesauri

TEACHING AID NO. 12

Single Effect: Suggested Excerpts

The source of Edgar Allen Poe's theory of "single effect" is his essay "The Philosophy of Composition" in *Selected Writings of Edgar Allen Poe*, edited by Edward H. Davidson, (Cambridge, Massachusetts: The Riverside Press), 1956.

Mood	Excerpt
lighthearted	Paragraphs 3 & 4, Chapter 38, *Sweet Thursday*, John Steinbeck
drowsy to festive	Paragraph 2, "The Boys' Ambition," *Huckleberry Finn*, Mark Twain
tense, controlled	the wounded lion in the grass or the charging buffalo in "The Short Happy Life of Francis Macomber," Ernest Hemingway
foreboding	Paragraph 1, "The Fall of the House of Usher," Edgar Allan Poe
analytical, scientific	Paragraph 1, "The Murders in the Rue Morgue," Edgar Allen Poe
insane	Second-to-last paragraph, "The Tell-Tale Heart," Edgar Allan Poe*

*This work is short enough to record in its entirety.

Teaching Sequence

1. Review sensory description and connotation.
2. Introduce Edgar Allan Poe, his style, and his theory of "single effect" (see Teaching Aid No. 12). As a class, look over a Poe selection and pick out diction that promotes the prevailing mood or effect.
3. Tell the students you will play a number of story excerpts. Ask them to listen closely. Then play the recordings, pausing after each to discuss its prevailing mood.
4. Play the recordings again but, this time, ask students to list words from each selection that create its particular effect. Discuss the words the students have recorded.
5. Brainstorm additional words evincing the same moods. When the class has exhausted its ideas, check a thesaurus for more suggestions.
6. Break into small groups and have each group appoint a scribe. Assign each group a mood or emotion (see Teaching Aid No. 13) or allow them to choose one of their own. Then have each group brainstorm nouns, verbs, and modifiers that would help develop that mood. Finally, ask them to work their words into a single effect paragraph of at least five sentences.
7. Circulate among the groups and supervise where necessary. Give aid where the brainstorming is yielding words of only one part of speech or where paragraph form is lacking. When the groups have completed their paragraphs, ask one member from each group to read the group's paragraph aloud.

Teaching Notes

• The recordings will be more interesting to the students if they are in a voice other than the teacher's. A voice (or voices) with which the students are unfamiliar is preferable; if the voice is tantalizingly familiar, the students will concentrate on identifying it, rather than on listening to what it's saying.
• Students generally prefer selecting their own single effect mood or emotion. Have a number of suggestions ready for the class but don't make them overly prescriptive.
• Some students may prefer to do the brainstorming and write the paragraph individually. Because of the personal nature of mood creation, they should be allowed to do so.
• Keep thesauri handy but encourage the students to search their own minds before referring to a thesaurus.

Suggested Moods and Emotions

Moods: relaxed, humorous, somber, frightened, nervous
Emotions: eagerness, jubilation, boredom, apprehension, tension, confusion, despair

• As a rule, the groups require some supervision to broaden their word search beyond just adjectives.
• The assignment is primarily a class interaction exercise, but the group work could be graded for originality and precision, and the students, for participation.

Variations

a. Incorporate visual art into the lesson by bringing, or having students bring, pictures and photos which suggest distinctive moods. As a class, examine some of the pictures for the mood they engender and brainstorm words of the same mood. Hand the rest of the pictures out randomly and have the students repeat the process individually on the pictures they receive.
b. Discuss how a descriptive use of color suggests mood. Link various colors to various moods, pointing out that mood varies even with the shades of a color. For example, in the red family, pink seems lighthearted, innocent, and young; rose seems seductive, and intense; and scarlet seems violent and passionate. Examine the use of color by such authors as Stephen Crane.

14 Mood Music

Because literature and music have many similarities as expressive arts, they may be studied together for a greater understanding of each. In this lesson, students are shown how the mood of a song is enhanced by the sound and connotations of its lyrics. Those who are musically talented are encouraged to extend the lesson to writing lyrics and music for songs.

Objectives

- Students learn that the sound of a word contributes to its emotional impact.
- Students relate music and literature as companion arts.

Materials

- recordings in which the mood of the music is carefully enhanced by its lyrics (see Teaching Aid No. 14)
- instrumental music (see Teaching Aid No. 14)

Teaching Sequence

1. Review *connotation*. Explain that the sound of a word also sometimes contributes to its meaning. Introduce and discuss the term *onomatopoeia*.
2. List for the class the vocal artists whose music you will be playing and discuss the concept of melding the mood of the music with the sound and sense of the lyrics.
3. Play the first song and discuss its prevailing mood. Let musically inclined students explain how the music creates the mood. Then play the song again, this time directing the students to record words that further enhance the feeling created by the music. As a class, discuss these responses and brainstorm additional words whose sound and sense create connotations.
4. Play the rest of the songs selected for the activity. Apply step 3 to each one.
5. Play a variety of instrumental music pieces, allowing time between selections for students to individually describe the mood of each piece and to list words or phrases they feel aptly describe that mood. Compare the results as a class.
6. Invite students to write their own musical scores and/or song lyrics for extra credit. The writing may be an individual or small group effort. Set aside a period for a recital of their original works.

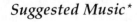

TEACHING AID NO. 14

*Suggested Music**

Mood	Music and Artist
light, airy	"The Lusty Month of May" *Camelot*, Warner Bros 1712
dreamlike, enchanting	"Follow Me" *Camelot*, Warner Bros 1712
longing, escapist	"El Condor Pasa" Simon & Garfunkel, *Bridge Over Troubled Water*, Columbia, KCS 9914
pressured	"The Big, Bright Green Pleasure Machine" Simon & Garfunkel, *Parsley, Sage, Rosemary, and Thyme*, Columbia CS 9363
dreamlike, fresh	"For Emily" Simon & Garfunkel, *Parsley, Sage, Rosemary, and Thyme*, Columbia CS 9363
jubilant	"Feelin' Groovy" Simon & Garfunkel, *Parsley, Sage, Rosemary, and Thyme*, Columbia CS 9363
pensive	"Cloudy" Simon & Garfunkel, *Parsley, Sage, Rosemary, and Thyme*, Columbia CS 9363
alienated, lost	"The Dangling Conversation" Simon & Garfunkel, *Parsley, Sage, Rosemary, and Thyme*, Columbia CS 9363
restless	"Gotta Move" Barbra Streisand, *Barbra Streisand's Greatest Hits*, Columbia KCS 9968
varied (instrumental)	*Stormy Weekend*. Mystic Moods Orchestra, Philips PHS 600-342
varied (instrumental)	*Grand Canyon Suite*. Leonard Bernstein and the New York Philharmonic, Columbia MS 6618

*Much of the music of the folk rock era is appropriate for this exercise. Because the message is the point of the genre, it tends to have clear diction and simple music. The themes generally appeal to young people.

Teaching Notes

• For the song analyses, popular music with which most students are familiar is acceptable. Using music with which they are unfamiliar, however, places them all on an equal footing and demonstrates that good music is music which speaks to people's common emotions.

• Allow at least half the period for step 5, because capturing the mood of a piece of music takes time. Insist upon quiet listening, so that distractions don't dispel the mood created by the music.

• The replay of songs in steps 3 and 4 can be eliminated by handing out copies of the lyrics. Doing so would diminish the effectiveness of the lesson as a mood study, however, because the students would be concentrating on reading, rather than on listening and feeling.

Variations

a. If the class demonstrates interest and maturity in the original activity, expand it to include written free association to instrumental music. Include a variety of themes and allow the interested students to stretch the exercise to poetry or prose writing.

b. Combine the lesson with classroom literature studies, examining prose and poetry for its mood-producing sound and rhythm qualities. For example, the same literary pieces suggested for activity 13, Single Effect, (see Teaching Aid No. 12), could be examined for their musical qualities. Discuss what properties make a word sound jubilant, tense, ponderous, gloomy, or scientific and then extend the analysis to sentence, paragraph, or overall structure.

15 Hard Sell Commercial

The radio students listen to, the TV they watch, and the magazines they read constantly bombard them with advertising propaganda; yet students often do not analyze, or even question, what they hear or see. In this lesson, they study both straightforward and misleading advertising and learn the techniques of persuasion by writing their own advertisements.

Objectives

- Students consider the subconscious effects of advertising propaganda and analyze its properties.
- Students practice concise, persuasive writing.
- Students utilize nonliterary skills in the English classroom.

Materials

- taped or videotaped advertisements from radio or TV
- advertisements clipped from magazines
- copies of Max Shulman's "Love is a Fallacy" (from *Studies in Prose Writing*, 3rd edition, Lee Cogan (New York: Holt, Rinehart and Winston, Inc.), 1974)

Teaching Sequence

1. As a class, read and discuss Max Shulman's "Love is a Fallacy." Make a list of the common fallacies of logic and keep the list available for the remainder of the activity.

2. Bring samples or recordings of persuasive advertising to class. Point out individual words and images that help inspire people's good feelings about the products. If there are inexact words that seem to promise results but actually do not, point those out, too. Also draw attention to any violations of logic. (see Teaching Aid 15)

3. Require students to bring in at least one sample each of misleading advertising. Have each student present an ad to the class and comment on any violated logic or empty language.

4. For a writing exercise, have students choose and write one of the following:

   - a script for a 30- to 60-second TV commercial, complete with a description of the visual portion of the message
   - a script for a 30- or 60-second radio commercial, complete with background music or sounds
   - a magazine advertisement of at least 120 words, complete with an illustrated or graphically designed background or a description of the background

Stress that the script, not the artwork or music, is the primary focus of the assignment.

5. If time and/or class requirements permit, have the students present their ads to the class and discuss the impact of each. Radio and TV commercial spots may be taped or videotaped and magazine ads dittoed for extra credit.

TEACHING AID NO. 15

Some Suggested Guidelines
for Spotting Misleading Ads

1. Ads that suggest a person will be young (or young-looking), beautiful, or shapely from merely using a product are making a hasty generalization based on the fact that an actor, actress, or model has the desirable quality and also uses the product. Soft drink and face cream ads often use this approach.

2. Ads that suggest a person will belong to the group, have fun, and be happy ("Be a Pepper") are bypassing the real reasons individuals are accepted by the crowd or are happy and are assigning popularity to the use of a product.

3. Circulars or junk mail that claim a person's name was specially selected and is one of a very few chosen should be suspect. Statistics about the multitude of such "very few lucky persons" receiving the mail will reveal the claim's insincerity.

4. Products bearing such spectacular titles as "Wonder" Such-and-Such or "Miracle" This-or-That always should be carefully scrutinized for the details. Somewhere in small print there will be an indication of how the miracle works, but this information will not be immediately noticeable. For example, an ad for a "Miracle Flashlight" that doesn't require batteries may reveal, after much perusal, that the light must be pumped to activate a generator—an action that certainly would make efficient use of the light beam difficult.

5. Background pictures (as in cigarette ads, for example) often make mute promises of how a person will look, perform, or feel after the use of a product. There is no logical connection whatsoever between the use of the product and the desirable appearance, performance, or feeling.

6. Some ads make claims that are impossible, or have contradictory premises. For example, if all aspirin has five grains of that pain reliever per tablet because it is the legal limit, none can be more *potent* regardless of size or extra ingredients.

7. Key phrases in radio or TV commercials are "What you need is . . . ," "You should have . . . ," "You need . . . ," "You want . . . ," "Get a . . . ." Such phrases program the listeners, creating wants and needs literally out of thin air.

8. Ambiguous phrases such as "may help" or "has been known to help" are misleading. They merely state a possibility.

Teaching Notes

• Be sure to include responsible, forthright ads as well as misleading or illogical ones so that a comparison may be made.

• Grade the written work for the subtle, persuasive use of words or images, or for deceptively imprecise wording.

• While the assignment has general appeal, it is especially enjoyed by the students with electronic or artistic talents. Remind the students that persuasive language, not audiovisual effects, is the purpose of the assignment.

Variations

a. Amass a stack of both responsible and misleading ads. Hand them out at random and challenge the students to critique them for directness, logic, and honesty.

b. As a follow-up or as an alternative to the original writing assignment, ask the students to write ads for utterly worthless or completely ridiculous items, such as a display cannister for crumpled candy wrappers or a pincushion for football spikes.

CHAPTER 5 Cruise to Clarity

16 Newscript

Scripts for radio and TV news reports are excellent models for precise and colorful diction. They are familiar to the students and are easily taped for classroom use. In addition, they demonstrate the difference between stories that entertain and stories that inform.

Objectives

- Students study and imitate the clean, clear style of TV and radio newscript writers.
- Students use a thesaurus.

Materials

- tape recording or videotape of radio and TV news programs
- thesauri

Teaching Sequence

1. Explain the restrictions under which news and sports writers must function, citing such things as the short amount of time allotted for each item, the need for sufficient synonyms to avoid monotony, and the number of details that must be clearly and logically presented.
2. Play the recording through once just for listening.
3. Play the recording again, asking the students to jot down (a) synonyms used for repeated terms or ideas, (b) especially colorful or appropriate descriptions, (c) high-content words or phrases that say much in little space.
4. Discuss the listings made in step 3. Have a list of your own prepared before class to aid in the discussion.
5. As a class, select a current events item, a school occurrence, or an historic event and write a one-minute newscript about it. Use precise diction and present all the necessary ideas logically. Use a thesaurus to find alternate expressions for the subject of the item so that repetition is avoided.
6. Assign each student a news item to be written up as a one- or two-minute newscript. Stress the importance of clear, logical, grammatical coverage. See that the students have access to a thesaurus.

7. On the due date, have the students present their items orally in a mock live news program. If possible, videotape the program.

Teaching Notes

• Point out the difference between entertaining fiction, which takes the time for small details and lengthy descriptions, and informative writing, which presents facts succinctly. Discuss the justifications for each style.
• Emphasize that logical presentation is often a matter of the proper coordination and subordination of ideas. Preparatory exercises in that area of grammar may be helpful.
• Warn the students against the temptation to write hastily and superficially because the assignment is short. Restate the importance of careful word choice and grammatical structure.
• Grade the items on precision, succinctness, and grammar.

Variations

a. Base the exercise on a literary or historic period. Have the students research news events of the time for their newscripts.
b. Base the exercise on the era encompassed by a particular literary work or base it on events within the work itself. Have the students research their items.
c. Expand the lesson to include the legal boundaries of journalism, discussing how news items may be slanted or poorly supported by facts. If possible, have a script writer or a reporter speak to the class. Then require the students to write a pair of scripts on a single news event—one script slanted or inaccurate, and the other objective and well-supported.
d. Limit the lesson to feature stories, which allow the writer more descriptive and interpretative freedom but still require precise and economical diction. Set a word limit if the article is to be written only, and a time limit if it is to be read aloud.
e. Phone a local radio or TV broadcasting station which features a regular news program. Request that the news department put aside a day's worth of Teletype news reports which have come over the wire from the various wire services (UPI, AP, Reuters). The used Teletype print-out will otherwise be discarded, so most stations are happy to save it for anyone who will pick it up promptly. Examine the print-out with the class. Then have each student select a news item and write an article from the raw data supplied on the print-out. Working from the

Teletype reports will lend an air of professionalism to the students' efforts.

17 Role Letters

Letter writing is a skill virtually all students will need in their practical adult lives. In this activity, students probe and assume adult roles, projecting possible occasions for writing business letters. Then they write letters to fit the occasions, practicing the clarity, organization, and tact which facilitate accurate communication.

Objectives

- Students develop writing skills in a credible context.
- Students learn business letter format.
- Students practice presenting ideas clearly and logically.

Materials

- sample correspondence chart for the class discussion (see Teaching Aid No. 16)

Teaching Sequence

1. Go over the attributes of well-written letters. Use examples, if possible, stressing the need for simple, clear expression. Explain verbiage and why excess words are especially bad in communications. Discuss tact and positive approach.
2. Discuss the circumstances in which adults must write letters, using the sample correspondence chart to initiate the discussion (see Teaching Aid No. 16). As a class, brainstorm additional occasions and record them on the board.
3. As a class, create an imaginary city. Name it and determine its population, location, and major businesses. Have each student create an imaginary individual who lives in the city. Encourage students to represent as many as possible of the different consumer and service roles likely to exist in that city.
4. On the board, make a three-columned chart with the headings *sender*, *topic*, and *receiver*. List the people and roles created

TEACHING AID NO. 16

Sample Corresponding Chart

SENDER	TOPIC	RECEIVER
homeowner	stray dog complaint	dogcatcher
dogcatcher	information on new tax form	IRS agent
grocer	appointment to discuss loan	banker
banker	need for new equipment	manufacturer
student	appointment for job interview	grocer
manufacturer	announcement of job opening	employment center
IRS agent	announcement of audit	homeowner
consumer	complaint about faulty order	catalog store
catalog store	collection letter	consumer
employment center	job listings for the month	student

by the class under *sender*. Then as a group, decide what reason each person might have for writing to some other person on the list. Place the reasons under *topic* and the recipients under *receiver* to complete the chart. (see Teaching Aid No. 16)

5. Introduce the parts and organization of business letters.

6. Have each student write a letter on the topic assigned his or her character and address it to the designated recipient. Allow out-of-class time on the assignment so that students may do whatever research is necessary to learn the nuances of their roles and topics. Set a due date by which all letters must be "posted" (brought to class).

7. "Deliver" the letters in class. Then assign responses to the letters and set a new due date.

8. After the responses are delivered, ask the students to answer the following questions about both the letters and the replies they have received:
- Can you completely understand the letter? If not, why not? In the case of the reply letter, could the error have arisen from a lack of clarity in your original correspondence? If so, correct your original letter.
- Are there unnecessary words or phrases burdening the letter? If so, list some.
- Did the letter writer get right to the point?
- Was the writer tactful? How did you feel when you read the letter?

9. Collect the letters and critiques for grading.

Teaching Notes

- Help the students research the roles they choose. Arrange field trips to businesses or ask secretaries or businesspeople to speak to the class. Help set up individual interviews for students who choose topics requiring knowledge of a particular service or product.
- Grade the letters on clarity, organization, form, and content. Review the critiques for additional insight on your students' abilities to self-edit and on the level of their understanding.

Variations

a. The planning session in steps 3 and 4 is a good motivational method, but it may be eliminated to save time. Instead of conducting a planning session, merely present the students with a list of roles and start the discussion of who will write to whom for what reason.

b. Expand the lesson to include, or even emphasize, the persuasive letter. Examine sample letters of persuasion and discuss their pattern of arousing interest, creating desire, convincing the reader, and urging the reader to act. Brainstorm occasions for writing such letters (see Teaching Aid No. 17). Then either include persuasive topics on the sender-topic-receiver chart or use such topics exclusively. Expand the critique list used in step 8 to include questions pinpointing the qualities of good persuasive writing:
- Was the action you were asked to take clearly defined? If dates, places, and times were involved, were they clearly presented?

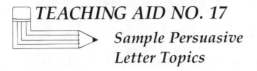

TEACHING AID NO. 17
Sample Persuasive Letter Topics

1. Assume you are the secretary of a club or the manager of a team. Invite a specialist in your field to speak at an annual banquet.
2. Write a form letter arousing interest in the formation of a special interest club such as a jogging, rifle, Bible, or handiwork club.
3. Request your city maintenance department to install a particular road sign (speed limit, slow, stop) on your street.
4. Write a form letter arousing interest in a neighborhood project to clean up a vacant lot that is an eyesore or a safety hazard.
5. Write your car insurance company with suggestions for simplifying their claim form.

- Did the action seem to be in your best interests? Was it made as easy as possible for you to take such an action?
- Did the conclusion of the body of the letter encourage you to take action? Did it make you understand why you should act promptly?

18 Office Communications

Because most students will eventually have to fill out business forms and write memos on the job, the study of interbusiness communications in English class is justified. In this lesson, students study various types of office and fieldwork forms and practice completing them clearly, completely, and succinctly. Local businesses serve as resources.

Objectives

- Students study forms used by businesses for which they may work in the future.

- Students appreciate the practical application of English skills.
- Students practice clear and logical explanatory writing.

Materials

- samples of communications forms from local businesses (memos, field reports, purchase orders, lab reports, telephone message forms, accident reports, periodic reports, and others)
- duplicated forms for student use
- a communications chart (see Teaching Aid No. 18)

Teaching Sequence

1. Use the various communication forms to create a flow chart of business communications on the bulletin board.

2. Go over the flow chart with the students, explaining how each form is used and where its copies go.

3. Discuss good writing style for these forms—precise and logical, with no wasted words and no information left out. Read some samples from a technical writing text or use an actual business correspondence to demonstrate the correct style.

4. As a class, create an imaginary organization with as many roles for individuals as there are students in the class. On the board, make a three-columned chart with the headings *sender*, *topic*, and *receiver*. List the individual roles under *sender*. Then, as a group, decide what type of correspondence each person is likely to send to another person on the list or to an outside supplier or associate. Place the type of correspondence under *topic* and the recipients of the correspondence under *receiver* on the chart. Label outside recipients as being in the field, factory, branch office, or a tangentially related organization. Label in-house recipients with their organizational functions. (see Teaching Aid No. 18)

5. Assign each student one sender role and one receiver role from the chart. Have students use the appropriate format to communicate their topic information. Set a due date for the forms.

6. Deliver the forms in class and have the students critique the forms on the following points:
- Is the message clear? Are you sure what your subsequent action should be?
- Did the message come right to the point?

TEACHING AID NO. 18

Sample Communications Chart

SENDER	TOPIC	RECEIVER
typist	purchase order	supply company
stockperson	message to line repairperson to conserve gloves, which are low in stock	line repairperson
line repairperson	report on trouble-shooting	overseer
overseer	periodic report on repairs	board of directors
president	arrangements for a production meeting	vice president, branch office
head secretary	description of new forms to be used in all offices	all typists

- Were there useless words in the message? If so, list some.
- Was the communication tactful? How did you feel when you read it?
  7. Collect the forms and the critiques for grading.
  8. Have the students exchange roles and repeat the exercise.

Teaching Notes

• Step 2 may include guest speakers from local businesses. Such people lend credibility to the activity and offer insights into the intricacies of interoffice paperwork.

• The exercise should be repeated at least once to give students experience with as many forms as possible.

• Grade the forms on precision, clarity, and tact. Look over the critiques for further manifestation of individual students' understanding.

Variation

Limit the activity to such common types of business forms as memos, telephone message reports, and accident reports. Samples of these forms should be available in your school. Eliminate step 4 and go directly from the discussion to the assignment of one completed form of each type per student.

19 Burning Deadwood

Always afraid of coming up short on words, students fill in their compositions with lifeless spaceholders, or *deadwood*. In this exercise, they receive padded writing samples from the instructor and proceed to red pen—"burn out"—phrases of low information content. They also rewrite passive constructions into active ones. Then they repeat the techniques on written work of their own.

Objectives

• Students learn which common phrases or words signal verbiage in their writing.
• Students learn to recognize and change passive constructions.
• Students attempt to write without using deadwood or excessive passives.

Materials

• a list of deadwood and hackneyed expressions (see Teaching Aid No. 19)
• sample written works choked with deadwood and/or passive constructions (see Teaching Aid No. 20)
• grammar exercises for changing passive verbs to active ones

Teaching Sequence

1. Define and discuss *deadwood, hackneyed phrases,* and *clichés.* Provide a sample list of these literary deadbeats and have the students brainstorm to add to it. Discuss the simple words that can replace many deadwood phrases. (see Teaching Aid No. 19).

2. Discuss passive construction and provide examples of wishy-washy, passive sentences rewritten as strong, active ones. Do an exercise from a grammar text to further demonstrate the principle.

3. As a class, do the sample rewrite included in this activity. Copy the article without the underlining, and let the students pick out the abundant deadwood (see Teaching Aid No. 20).

4. Hand out copies of several compositions that contain deadwood and abundant passive verbs, giving the students time to burn out the verbiage and rewrite the weak verbs. Select students to read their two versions aloud for class discussion.

5. Assign a composition in keeping with the writing program for the class. Stress that burning out deadwood is an integral part of the revision, and require the students to hand in their red-penned rough copies as well as their finished papers.

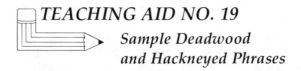

TEACHING AID NO. 19

Sample Deadwood and Hackneyed Phrases

Deadwood (with simple replacement words in parentheses)
being that (since)
in order that (so)
due to the fact that (because)
in the area [vicinity] of (near, around)
it is necessary to (one must, you must)
for a period of (for)
for the purpose of (for, to)
in relation to (concerning)
came to the conclusion that (concluded, decided)
in the course of (during)
made an attempt at (attempted, tried)

Hackneyed Phrases

sad but true	you just can't help
wouldn't you know	last but not least
you know	first and foremost
you never can tell	in the long run
it goes to show	when all is said and done
around about	going on to say

Due to the fact that the baseball *had been put away* by his mother, Bill couldn't find it in his room *subsequent to* his walk home from school. He searched *in the vicinity of* his cluttered desk and all around his room *in order to* locate it but finally *came to the conclusion that* it *was not to be found by* him. *For the purpose of* showing his anger, he stomped around his room *for a period of* a few minutes, *during which time* several drawers and his closet door *were slammed by* him. Then he burst from his room *by way of* the door and clattered down the stairs and through the house *in an effort to* get to the back door. *It was necessary for him to* reach up for his cap and mitt on the shelf *in the area of* the door, and when he did so, the baseball, which was also there, *was knocked off the shelf by* his finger tips. *As a result*, he saw it. He *made a* laugh that sounded jubilant, *took a* swipe *in order to* catch the rolling ball, and crashed out the back door *on his way toward* the gang on the sand-lot.

Sample Revision

Because his mother had put his baseball away for him, Bill couldn't find it in his room when he got home after school. He dug through the clutter on his desk and searched his room, finally deciding it just wasn't there. Angry, he stomped around the room for a few minutes, slamming the drawers and his closet door. Then he burst from his room, clattered down the stairs, and tore through the house to the back door. He reached up for his cap and mitt, which were on a high shelf by the door; and his groping fingers dislodged the baseball resting beside them. He laughed jubilantly when he saw it fall, then swept it up, and bolted out the back door to join his friends on the sand-lot.

Teaching Notes

• For step 4, use as many examples of deadwood-choked pieces of writing as possible. Student papers from former years are a good source if the names are removed from the papers. Some composition textbooks have sample wordy paragraphs, as do many technical writing manuals. Some technical writing manuals also supply comprehensive lists of phrases that carry little information.

• Grade the homework composition for clarity and freedom from verbiage. Base the grade partly on the efforts made to edit useless words from the rough draft.

Variation

Have the students write paragraphs including as much deadwood as possible. Then let them exchange papers in pairs to red pen the deadwood and passive verbs in each other's work. Allow time at the end of the period for them to return the papers and discuss with the authors the items they edited.

CHAPTER 6 Explore Points of View

20 Starship Radio Message

The Starship Radio Message is an appealing format for a short, intense writing assignment. From the perspective of an alien creature, students record their first impressions of Earth in a precise, descriptive report to their home planet. Such a scenario encourages them to view familiar surroundings objectively and to reinterpret them logically in their writings.

Objectives

- Students practice writing sensory description.
- Students learn to infer conclusions by carefully examining material.

Materials

- scenarios in which an alien encounters life on Earth (see Teaching Aid No. 21)
- art supplies for illustration (optional)

Teaching Sequence

1. Review sensory description.
2. Explain to the class that each of them is to be a creature from another planet who is visiting Earth for the first time. Each is obligated to report to a commander in another starship or on the home planet, recording briefly his or her first impressions of Earth.
3. Provide a sample scenario as a hand-out or a board presentation. Include some variables that will affect the creature's responses, such as the alien's physical makeup, the social or physical characteristics of its home planet, and the place and season of its Earth landing. Give the students the option of creating their own scenario (see Teaching Aid No. 21).
4. Stress the importance of brevity in the writing. The radio message must not be intercepted; the more quickly it can be transmitted through space, the less likely it will be traced and decoded by earth scientists. Encourage each student to make every word count in two or three paragraphs of revealing description.

TEACHING AID NO. 21

Sample Scenarios

1. You are from Grasperon, where all individuals look exactly alike. All of you have a ring of tentacles that spring from your waists in all directions, like an octopus, and a wheeled tripod instead of feet. Otherwise you resemble Earthlings. You have landed on the beach at Fort Lauderdale, Florida, during Easter vacation.

2. You are from Optimeron, where no one says anything negative about anyone or anything. The quality of work on your planet is poor, so your space vehicle and suit are less than perfect. You have landed in the Himalayas in a snowstorm.

Sample Radio Message
Starship Zinc to Optimeron

Come in Optimeron. We landed on Earth one glone ago, just after losing radio contact with you. At landing our thermogig registered −90° Z, then shattered. Atmospheric conditions have been remarkably static since then: the air is cold and white, as are the ground and sky. Pollution seems nonexistent; the air is too thick with ice particles to admit any other substances, and the wind velocity prevents odors from lingering. Such conditions would present an admirable challenge to homebuilders.

Space hero Antron has already been outside looking for Earth rocks to bring home. He performed splendidly, manipulating the probe with only two hands while holding his umbilical in its socket with the other. The umbilical became dislodged when the exit ladder self-destructed one hundred fifty glones early. The explosive mechanism operated perfectly, a true tribute to the quality of Optimeron's work force.

Antron looked splendid upon re-entry. His upper nose was a striking shade of blue but the lower one, both eyes, and his audio horn were normal. All eighteen fingers were still intact and only the twenty-third and twenty-fourth toes on his foot were lost. He reported no discomfort.

We will tabulate Antron's geological findings and transmit again in three glones. Zinc out.

5. Do one sample message as a class, outlining it on the board as it develops. If you have used sample scenario 2, compare the class's starship message to the sample radio message (see Teaching Aid No. 21). Then assign the writing of individual messages based on a new scenario devised by you or the class.
6. Provide art supplies for students to illustrate their messages *after* you have approved the work. Encourage interested students to illustrate their messages through sound, light, or other modes of expression.
7. Read aloud and post the more competent and original papers. Discuss how writers inadvertently reveal a great deal about themselves through their recorded observations of other people and things. Note the inferences, beyond those specified in the scenarios, that can be made about the "aliens" who wrote the papers presented in class.

Teaching Notes

• Exercise the art option only after the students' writing has met with your approval. The radio messages should be precise and descriptive enough to communicate without visual aids. Do not allow the art to become the object of the assignment.
• Evaluate the writings on originality, conciseness, logic, consistency, and the mechanics of composition. Allow extra credit for effective artwork.

Variations

a. Rather than providing all the variables in the original scenario, leave some of the creative responsibility to the students. Either provide the basic information about the alien and its planet, or select the landing place of the starship. The students will fill in the missing variables and thus create more diversified messages.
b. If class response to the original plan is enthusiastic, do a follow-up in which each student hands in both an original scenario and a radio message. During the next class meeting, "intercept" the messages by reading them aloud in class. Challenge the class members to infer information about the alien and its planet and record the inferences on the board. Then read the actual scenarios for comparison.
c. If your students are enthusiastic after the first assignment,

follow up with a new premise. Tell the class that two months have elapsed since the original message, and a new report home is due. Discuss how they will have had time to experience night and day as well as some seasonal changes, to travel about their immediate area and observe new phenomena, and to watch or interact with Earthlings. Remind them that brevity and precise content are more important than ever.

d. Use the radio message as an introduction to science fiction. Discuss how writers of science fiction and fantasy create a universe intentionally different from our own and then follow the rules of that universe exclusively. Readers learn to function in the new setting the same way they do in real life—by generalizing patterns from related incidents—and they are often fooled, delighted, and surprised in the process. Assign the reading of one or two short science fiction stories to illustrate the point. "Harrison Bergeron" (Kurt Vonnegut, Jr.) or "Smith of Wootton Major" (J.R.R. Tolkien) are two possibilities.

e. Use the assignment as an introduction to character creation, in general, pointing out how readers learn about characters by what they do, think, and say, just as the class learned about the aliens from their messages. Have the class read a short story, such as "The Black Cat" (Edgar Allan Poe) or "Flight" (John Steinbeck). Discuss the story, outlining on the board the facts learned about the character's physical and mental makeup, background, and location. Follow up with an imitative writing assignment.

21 Personification

Personification is an exceptionally versatile writing assignment that appeals to all ages and elicits from each the greatest possible maturity of perception. The students are asked to select an object, determine its environment and responses, and then work the information into a first person account from the viewpoint of the object. The process provokes clear, logical thinking and some very perceptive descriptive writing in both humorous and serious veins. Students generally enjoy sharing the results as a class.

TEACHING AID NO. 22

Sample Personification

Running Shoes

I can hardly believe it! Someone is going to buy me and take me out of this stuffy box and this dive of a shoe store to see the real world! At last I'll have a chance to run as I was designed to do, to fleet over miles of terrain, or to rip down all-weather tracks to new records in racing speed. I will be a credit to my manufacturer!

My owner is opening the box again. We met only briefly in the store; now perhaps we'll go for a run and become better acquainted. I'll prove to her my light construction and waffled sole make me superior to all other shoes. She already knows I'm better looking. I don't know how any runner can resist my distinctive blue color, especially highlighted as it is with yellow racing stripes. I'm surprised my manufacturer has any competition left.

She's lacing me up now, quickly and efficiently, right through the tongue without hesitation. I think this girl has handled running shoes before. That means I'll soon be bent double to hasten my limbering up . . . yes, she's going to do it now . . . ooooh, that does stretch one's fibers. Now, on to the feet . . . hey, clean, soft, sweat socks! They must be new; I wonder if we are from the same store? The feet inside them feel funny. The toes poke and have hard places on them. I wonder if my cushions and supports will have any resilience left when we are done today. I hope this gal doesn't run marathons . . . oh, here we go!

What's this stuff? Why are we running on this rocky sand when there's pavement just to the side of us: This must be the road shoulder that we were told of in the factory. It's just my luck to get an owner who believes in roughing it. Ah, well, she still has a good style: graceful strides, long and even. All right! Let's burn those miles! Lift those knees! Reach! Reach!

What's that smell? Aaugh, is that foot odor? They said it would be bad, but this is obnoxious. Gasp. Yes, it must be foot odor; here's the perspiration. I'd better get busy and absorb it as I'm supposed to. At least I'm still dry on the outside. I'm sure we'd never go in any mud or water, would we?

Continued on next page.

We would. Gad, what slop. She must be used to this because she doesn't even break stride. We must be training for an important race to go at it this seriously. Well, they never said that being a champion would be easy. On, lady runner! I'm with you all the way!

Objectives

- Students practice sensory description and first person composition.
- Students employ logical reasoning to view their world from other perspectives.
- Students study point of view.

Materials

- sample personification (see Teaching Aid No. 22)
- list of ideas and guidelines (see Teaching Aid No. 23)

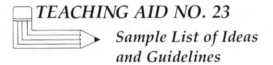

TEACHING AID NO. 23

Sample List of Ideas and Guidelines

a flag	a test paper
a ball	a sweat suit
a school desk	a record or tape
a body of water	an animal, bird, or insect
a Christmas tree	a sound speaker
a light switch	a match
a doorknob	a musical instrument
a textbook	

1. Where is this object?
2. What can it see, hear, smell, touch, taste?
3. What is its attitude—sulky, energetic, critical, conceited, optimistic?
4. What unusual thing could happen to it?

Teaching Sequence

1. Define *personification* and read a sample (see Teaching Aid No. 22).

2. Discuss first person writing and point of view. As a class, rewrite the personification from another point of view. Note how the point of view must be consistent, drawing only upon knowledge the object would have.

3. List on the board some sample ideas. Discuss one or two in depth, asking guiding questions to establish the object's perception. (see Teaching Aid No. 23)

4. Assign the writing of a personification based upon one of the listed ideas or permit students to come up with their own ideas. Encourage the students to spend time brainstorming their topics and responses before beginning to write. Suggest that those who have chosen objects they are able to observe do so before writing.

5. Read or post the more perceptive personifications as a basis for a follow-up discussion.

Teaching Notes

• Stress that point of view limits what an object knows. The object's experiences and environment must be carefully considered before writing commences.

• Circulate and help, particularly with younger students, as the students brainstorm. Be sure the students complete a list of ideas based upon the guiding questions before starting to write.

• Grade on originality and depth of perception as well as on the elements of good composition.

Variations

a. Correct and return the personifications, reading the more perceptive ones in class and using them as a basis for a follow-up discussion. Then assign another personification from the point of view of a closely related object. As an example, outline the feeling of the runner about the shoe in the sample personification. Point out that the runner would know what goal was being pursued as well as why running on gravel and through mud was necessary. She would also have some response to the shoe's appearance and performance. Allow the students to begin working in class and circulate to advise them

in their choice of a counter point of view. Read or post the pairs of papers that show the greatest originality and perception.
b. Conduct the follow-up discussion and make the assignment in variation *a*, but have the students exchange papers and write the opposing point of view for someone else's paper.

22 This Was the Year

This Was the Year is an exercise in parallelism, the logical combination of ideas, and point of view. Students are separated into small groups, asked to record reminiscences of the past school year, and then told to combine similar ideas into sentences beginning "This was the year. . . ." The students must use parallel structure within each sentence to relate these similar ideas. The activity allows them to examine everyday school life for its story content and to see the patterns into which their individual experiences fit.

Objectives

- Students use parallel structure to combine related ideas into one sentence.
- Students study writing from a specific point of view.

Materials

- copies of "This Was the Year" (see Teaching Aid No. 24)

Teaching Sequence

1. Read through "This Was the Year," a prose poem (see Teaching Aid No. 24).
2. Discuss the point of view from which the poem was written. Ask for suggestions of other points of view from which the same material could be written—teacher's or librarian's, for example—and rewrite one or two items from those points of view.
3. Discuss parallel structures and take apart several sentences from the poem to examine their internal parallel parts. Point

TEACHING AID NO. 24

"This Was The Year" Exercise

This was the year when we all came very fresh to KCHS and proved it by wandering into classes made up of juniors and seniors and by calling teachers by the wrong names and by being generally embarrassed. This year the school seemed huge at first and then seemed to shrink every day as we became used to it.

This was the year when some teachers were fun and some were strict and when the librarian was always strict about our paying our fines and not chewing gum.

This was the year of algebra, which always does things the hard way, and of P. E., which makes five cals seem like twenty.

This was the year of the hot lunch program. This year we stood in line for twenty minutes and then spent our lunch money on milk shakes and pop when the balanced diet was "slop."

This was the year of initiation, of dressing up like baby dolls and eating baby food, of munching onion sandwiches, of getting to give a senior a piggyback ride.

This was the year when new privileges led students to try out the tardy and skip rules, to get suspended, and to think about it. This year the gambling in the restrooms made nature's call a real difficulty.

This was the year of fire alarms that at first were fun but later were very cold.

This was the year that Karl got a haircut.

This was the year that wasn't fun but really was, the year that we were "babies" but really weren't, the year that we started out hating but ended up loving.

out the overall parallelism achieved by starting each sentence or group with the same words.

4. Talk briefly about nostalgia and the human tendency to glamorize school days or other "good old days." Ask the students for some of their memories from when they were five or eight years younger.

5. Divide the class into small groups of mixed ability. Challenge the groups to brainstorm experiences from their present and recent past that will one day be their fond memories. Stress that every idea should be recorded in the initial brainstorming session and that the less important ones can be eliminated later. Point out that a few bad experiences should be included because such happenings mellow out to humorous memories over the years. Set a time limit for the session.

6. When the brainstorming session is over, set another time limit and have the students pick out the best twenty ideas from their lists. Encourage them to include some suggestions from each member of the group.

7. When the list is finished, give the groups another time limit for grouping the ideas into small, related experiences. Circulate and help during this step.

8. Direct the students to write sentences beginning "This was the year. . ." into which they combine the related ideas. Warn them against overloading a sentence and point out how some of the entries in the original exercise run to two sentences. Stress that structure within each entry must be parallel.

9. Post the results.

Teaching Notes

• Designate work groups of mixed ability. The less capable students will be helped by the others in the difficult business of parallelism.

• Be sure to check with each group periodically, especially during the writing stage, to keep the activity on target and to guide the students. Each group will need help or reminders to keep the verbs in the same tense and the structures parallel.

• The assignment is essentially a nongraded drill, but group grades could be assigned on the basis of parallelism, consistency of point of view, and logical combination of ideas.

• Rather than posting individual group papers, try combining the class's efforts into one long list. Hand out copies and suggest the students file them away for a few years and reread them when they are older.

Variations

a. Brainstorm memories and select twenty ideas as a class instead of in small groups. Then form groups and have each one approach the same experience from a different point of view.

For example, different groups could describe the same event from the viewpoint of the principal, the janitor, the school bleachers, the school mascot, or even the school building itself.

b. Follow the teaching sequence as outlined but have the student groups all assume the point of view of someone or something bizarre, like the basketball hoop or the coach's whistle, to be the storyteller. Once the point of view is established, discuss just what that person or object could know and experience. Then let the students begin the group work.

c. For an additional drill in parallelism, have the groups exchange finished prose poems and proofread the ones they receive for violations of parallelism. Work individually with the groups both before, and after, the exchange.

23 Open Endings

In this story-writing activity, students are given either partial stories to be completed or complete stories to be rewritten. To fulfill either assignment, they must examine the logic of character, plot, and point of view as well as exercise creativity to complete or change the story. The format is flexible enough to provide basic materials for all and freedom to invent for the gifted. It may easily be integrated with history or current events studies.

Objectives

- Students approach the same circumstances from differing points of view.
- Students examine the logic of story endings.
- Students review the elements of a story, especially the parts of a plot.

Materials

- short films or videotapes with a story format

Teaching Sequence

1. Show at least two films or videotapes almost all the way through, stopping before the major conflicts are resolved.

2. As a class, discuss the stories up to the stopping points. Determine the point of view in each and come up with brief character sketches. Determine the initial incident, conflict, and rising action, and decide what is necessary to finish the plot.

3. Discuss how a good story develops logically and how good characters remain consistent. Point out that the end of the story must be based upon the beginning and middle.

4. Ask the students to write an ending to one of the stories. Remind them to build upon what they have learned of the characters and situations in the story they choose and to maintain the point of view established at the beginning of that story.

5. If the writing is done in class, circulate and advise, especially among the less inventive students. Encourage creative students to seek inventive solutions to the conflicts in their stories.

6. Post the better endings or read them to the class. Play the tapes or films through to their actual endings for comparison.

Teaching Notes

• Endings may differ and still be valid. An inventive main character may resolve the conflict favorably several different ways, just as an incompetent one may botch it in as many.

• Finding TV material the students haven't seen is difficult. If TV must be used, make arrangements to tape daytime television reruns of old sitcoms or cuts of old movies.

• Provide at least two stories, or more if time permits, so students have ample material to choose from.

• Grade the papers for consistency of character and point of view, for logical story development, and for the elements of good composition.

Variations

a. Play the films or tapes all the way through. Expand the discussion in step 2 to include *turning points*, explaining how a change of one occurrence, response, or personality in the chain of events could result in many different endings. Discuss the vast number of choices an author has throughout the creative process.

Help the students find places in the stories where different actions by the characters could have changed the course of the entire story. Then assign a rewrite which follows one such change to a logical conclusion. Encourage capable students to seek their own turning points.

b. Play the films or tapes all the way through and discuss them in terms of point of view. Note the ways in which point of view affects every turning point in a story. Explain how the story could be told differently from another point of view and read a sample rewrite to demonstrate. Suggest some other viewpoints and assign a rewrite of one story from a differing point of view. Use the rewrites for a follow-up discussion on turning points.

c. Use news reports from the radio, TV, or the newspaper instead of film stories. Discuss the events thoroughly so that all the students are made aware of the cause-and-effect relationships within them. Then ask them to choose one news story and either rewrite it from a different point of view or change the ending by manipulating personalities, responses, or events in the story. This variation works well in conjunction with a current events program.

d. Instead of tapes or films, use stories from a literature or history text other than the one used in class. Hand out dittoed pages which leave off at a turning point. Invite students to complete the stories, perhaps changing literature or history in the process. Distribute the "real" turning point resolutions and compare.

e. If drama is incorporated in your English or creative writing program, the activity can be adapted to include a critical comparison of written and film versions of a single work of literature. The discussion should focus on how point of view and its impact may shift according to the interpretations of the directors and actors. The point may be demonstrated by stopping both the film and the reading at the same point and allowing the students to finish one or the other. Compare the students' film endings with their literary endings. Then compare the "real" film endings with the "real" literary endings. Two famous examples of films which change the endings of the literature from which they are adapted are *A Streetcar Named Desire* and *Bridge Over the River Kwai*.

24 Tales After Canterbury

Chaucer's *Canterbury Tales* provides an entertaining and stimulating format for this activity on point of view. The students examine the types of tales and the interrelationships of the storytellers in the masterpiece. Then they create a similar framework for a group writing project in which each student contributes a story written from a particular point of view.

Objectives

- Students encounter some of the characteristics of medieval literature.
- Students practice writing short stories from a specific point of view.

Materials

- a modern translation (tapes, if desired) of the General Prologue, at least two tales, and a transition from the *Canterbury Tales* (see Teaching Aid No. 25)
- a recording of Middle English poetry (optional) (see Teaching Aid No. 25)

Teaching Sequence

1. Introduce the *Canterbury Tales,* establishing its position in English literary history. Explain that an occasion for storytelling was once a common literary format, citing such other examples as Boccaccio's *Decameron* and the ancient Arabian tales of *The Thousand Nights and a Night.*

2. Read the tales aloud (or play the tape). Annotate the tales with any background material necessary for the class to appreciate those you have chosen for the activity.

3. Give a brief synopsis of several other stories from the masterpiece. Discuss how they reflect the interests and lifestyles of the period as well as the interrelationships among the pilgrims. Classify the tales according to the apparent intentions of their fictional storytellers.

- entertainment ("Wife of Bath's Tale")
- moralization ("Pardoner's Tale")
- satire or rivalry ("Summoner's Tale" and "Friar's Tale")
- revival of classical romance ("Knight's Tale")
- insight into the individual characters and the English social structure (all the tales)

4. Help the class plan a framework for their own set of tales (see Teaching Aid No. 26). Discuss the types of individuals who would make up the group and establish the rivalries,

TEACHING AID NO. 25

> Sources and Suggestions

Modern Translation

Chaucer, Geoffrey, *Canterbury Tales*, translated by J. U. Nicolson, illustrated by Rockwell Kent. Garden City Publishing Co., Inc.: Garden City, N. Y. 1934.

Suggested Recording in Middle English

Early English Poetry, Folkways Records and Service Corp., New York City, 1966.

Synopses of Suggested Tales

"The Manciple's Tale": a legend of why crows croak and are black

"The Franklin's Tale": an uplifting tale of honor in a love triangle

"The Nun's Priest's Tale": the fable of Chanticleer

"The Wife of Bath's Tale": a moralistic tale proving one is better off with a foul but true wife than with a fair but faithless one

"The Pardoner's Tale": a moralistic tale about three men who set out to kill Death but are undone by their own greed

"The Friar's Tale": rival tales, each about evil men in the
"The Summoner's Tale": other's profession

---

friendships, and general values of the group. Then let each student assume the role of one character and write a tale from that character's standpoint.

5. Review the elements of the short story and apply them to the sample tales from Chaucer. Note Chaucer's attention to the small details, such as personal habits, dress, and possessions, which help establish the social history of the fourteenth century as well as the idiosyncracies of individual characters. Recommend that the students include similar details. Also suggest that the students carefully define their characters for themselves before starting to write in order to establish a consistent point of view in the tale.

6. On the due date, let the students take turns reading their

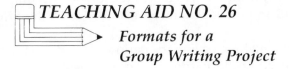

TEACHING AID NO. 26

Formats for a
Group Writing Project

1. students from a particular area of the U.S. on a long class trip by bus
2. students stranded in a dark school during a power shortage
3. assorted skiers snowbound in a chalet
4. tourists on a bicycle tour of Boston, Washington, D.C., or some other historic place
5. Senators or Representatives daydreaming during a congressional fillibuster.

tales aloud. Tales that were written in rivalry should be read back to back.

Teaching Notes

• Point out that Chaucer's tales are stories about individuals or groups. Warn the students against writing about the occasion for storytelling rather than writing a story. Chaucer's characters did not tell stories about pilgrims or pilgrimages; they drew instead from a variety of entertaining subjects.
• Not all the *Canterbury Tales* are appropriate for use in a high school. Preview the tales and select those appropriate for the level of maturity of the students and in keeping with the attitudes of the community. (see Teaching Aid No. 25)
• Modern translations of the tales are preferable because they save considerable reading and preparation time. The format and content of the work are being studied, not the language; however, a middle English recording may be included to add flavor and authenticity to the activity (see Teaching Aid No. 25).

Variations

a. Read one or more of the unfinished tales ("The Squire's Tale;" Chaucer's own rhymed tale) and challenge the students to finish one of these tales in a manner consistent with its beginnings.

b. Select a specific historic or literary period. Discuss its characteristics and allow the students to fabricate stories reflecting the social history and individual characterizations, as in the original activity.

c. Select a specific historic or literary period. Ask each student to pen a tale reflecting the nature and problems of an actual, prominent individual in that era.

25 Dramatic Dialogues

In Dramatic Dialogues, students learn that descriptive writing and story exposition need not follow a narrow format. They study how successful authors advance story action and provide essential background information through the conversations between their characters. These conversations also help establish the point of view from which the literature is written and the individual viewpoints of the characters. Attempting to imitate these dialogues forces the students to consider the underlying craft in dialogue. It also give them an opportunity to describe and interpret one of their own life experiences.

Objectives

- Students examine the part dialogue plays in successful story writing.
- Students write dialogue that reveals their characters' personalities and viewpoints and that advances story action.

Materials

- sample dialogues written by students or professional writers, taped if desired (see Teaching Aid No. 27)
- cassette recorders (optional)

Teaching Sequence

1. Read aloud, enact, or play recordings of the sample dialogues.
2. Discuss the dialogues, listing on the board all the information that may be gleaned from them about the speakers and

*Sources for
Dramatic Dialogues*

1. *The Brute*, Anton Chekhov (one-act play)
2. *The Stronger*, August Strindberg (one-act play)
3. *Mother and Child*, Langston Hughes (one-act play)
4. "Hills Like White Elephants," Ernest Hemingway (short story)
5. "Marriage a la Mode," Katherine Mansfield (short story)
6. "The Last Judgment," Karel Capek (short story)

their topic of conversation. Discuss how the story action is advanced by the speeches and how necessary background information is worked into them. Point out how the author's point of view is established by the types of dialogue tags attached to the speeches.

3. For a writing assignment, require a two- or three-page dialogue that tells a complete story. Specify that it should include only the speeches, no dialogue tags or expository paragraphs. Recommend that the students listen to classroom, lunchroom, or home conversations for inspiration if they have difficulty choosing a subject or scenario. If possible, make cassette recorders available so they may tape these conversations for reference. (see Teaching Aids No. 28 and No. 29)

4. Allow several days of homework time for the completion of the dialogues.

5. Share the more expressive and revealing conversations with the class, allowing the authors to assign parts to their classmates for an oral reading.

Teaching Notes

• Because the students will try to tell the story and describe the emotions in it through dialogue tags or brief expository paragraphs if they are allowed to use them, stress that there must be dialogue *only* in the writing assignment.

• One-act plays are the best models for this exercise. Within a very few pages they complete an entire action and provide all

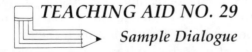

TEACHING AID NO. 28

Sample Dialogue
Scenarios

1. Two students talk about a dance or some other school event. One wants to go, the other doesn't. Details of the activity and the backgrounds and feelings of the speakers come out.
2. The captain of the debate team and the captain of the basketball team attend a school dance and see a fight in the parking lot. Each has a different version of the fight and different feelings about it as they discuss it the next day.
3. Two runners from different schools discuss their chances in the coming race, their physical readiness, their training, and their coaches. Each tries to "psych out" the other.
4. A parent and a small child talk about why the kitty or puppy can't eat at the table with the family.

TEACHING AID NO. 29

Sample Dialogue

Mom: Hi, Sweetie: Want a cookie? What did you do at school today?

Jason: Yeah! Nothin'.

Mom: Oh, come on now. You were there all day! What did you do just before you came home?

Jason: Let's see . . . oh, yeah! We picked up the books.

Mom: Oh? What books? Here's some milk.

Jason: The ones on the floor. Can't I have pop?

Mom: No. I suppose you were having reading time on the floor? Did you hear some good stories?

Jason: Nah, we didn't have reading time today. But seeing the books fall outa the bookcase was neater than stories.

Continued on next page.

Mom: I suppose so. How did that happen? Were you kids playing Star Wars again?

Jason: Uh uh! I think when the dog jumped over 'em he knocked 'em down. I wasn't watchin' that, I was watchin' the parakeet.

Mom: Hold on! What were a dog and parakeet doing in your classroom? Are you making up a story, Jason?

Jason: No, Mom! It was Zoo Day and kids brung

Mom: Brought! *Brung* isn't even a word!

Jason: Brought their pets. See, here's Captain Nimo in my pocket.

Mom: Oh, Zoo Day! I'll BET it was a zoo. A dog, a parakeet, a turtle, and 23 squirming first graders!

Jason: Yeah! Ya shoulda seen the parakeet! It was really neat when the cage fell over and it got out! It was peckin' Cindy an' she was hollerin' an' Miss Jacobs was tryin' to catch it 'til her fishbowl spilled. An' while she was rescuin' the fish, the cat ate the parakeet!!

Mom: Watch out for your milk! Fish, and a cat, too! Was the dog after the cat when it knocked over the bookcase?

Jason: Nah, they're both Jimmie's and they're pals. The dog was chasin' the chicken.

Mom: And the chicken was on the bookcase?

Jason: Yeah . . . No. Well, it was 'til it fell outa the window.

Mom: Wait a minute! What happened to the screen on the window?

Jason: Well, it sorta broke. Ya see, the bookcase fell when the dog jumped on it . . .

Mom: He must've been a big dog.

Jason: Yeah! He's a St. Bernard, an' he fell on the window and busted it an' then the chicken fell out, too.

Mom: I'll bet Miss Jacobs was glad to see them go! Poor lady.

Jason: I dunno. She was busy with Mickey. He was bawlin' about his parakeet that the cat ate. An' Becky was throwin' up cuz of the guts. That made two other kids throw up, too. It was neat!

Mom: You wouldn't have thought it was so neat if it had been your pet, or your tummy! But it all sounds even more interesting than TV. What else happened?

Jason: Nothin'; that's all. C'n I have another cookie?

Mom: No. You'd better put Captain Nimo away before you squash him. And wash your hands. I think that'll be the last Zoo Day for a while!

the background and characterization necessary to understand it.
• The dialogues should be graded on the amount of information and action presented in the speeches and on the plausibility of the situation created.

Variations

a. Discuss the three ways in which a playwright characterizes his or her players—by what other characters say about them, by what they say about themselves, and by their actions. Read the suggested one-act plays or some other dramatic pieces from the curriculum, analyzing them for character development through these three methods. Then assign the composition of a one-act play as a group writing project. Divide the class into two or three groups of no more than 10 students each. Instruct each group to write a short drama, with each character's speeches written by one pair or trio of students within the group. Require the groups to describe the characters and action in a précis to be approved by the teacher before they start writing the actual speeches.

b. Discuss characterization as in variation a, then assign the composition of a radio play, complete with sound effects. Caution the groups to make the speeches, not the sound effects, the object of the lesson. Arrange to have exceptional plays performed over the school's public address system for other classes to hear.

c. Allow the students to use dialogue tags and brief exposition to develop a distinct point of view for the story. Review the four main points of view (omniscient, limited omniscient, first person, direct observer) and the limitations of each.

d. Combine this lesson with activity 36, Speech Pattern Comparisons, for a more in-depth study of character development through dialogue.

CHAPTER 7 Soar with Description

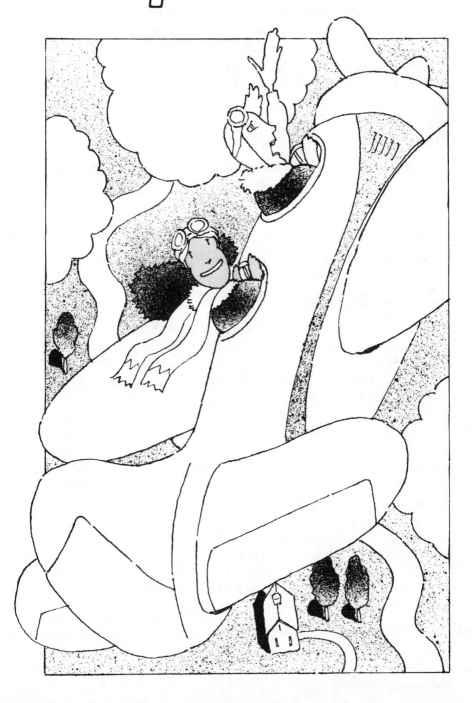

26 Communication Game

This TinkerToy® game is an excellent introduction to a writing course because it demonstrates clearly the difficulty of precise communication. Students take turns trying to direct their teammates to reproduce a model structure, working with certain handicaps. A follow-up discussion compares the activity to writing and accentuates the need for accuracy in any written communication.

Objectives

• Students experience the need for clear, accurate description.
• Students learn the relationship between writer and reader.

Materials

• a large set of TinkerToys® (put out by Child Guidance)

Teaching Sequence

1. Divide the group into as many pairs of A and B teams as possible depending on the number of TinkerToys available. Each pair of teams should have two identical sets of 15 to 20 TinkerToys. Ideally, all toy sets should be identical and each team should have only 2 or 3 members.

2. Direct each A team to build a structure using all its Tinker-Toys. When all the A groups are ready, invite one member of each B team to see its A team's structure. It is then that member's job to tell his or her B teammates how to reconstruct the model from their own set of toys. He or she must do so with the following handicaps:
   • Game 1—without the use of gestures
   • Game 2—without the use of verbal cues
   • Game 3—without restrictions

The scorekeeper is chosen from the A team and must watch the B member, deducting one point from B's starting score of 15 each time B uses a gesture or verbal cue. B may look at A's model as often as necessary, but no other member of the B team may see it. The first B group to accurately reproduce the A model gets 3 points to add to the number remaining from their starting score of 15. When all the structures have been completed, the scores are recorded on the chalkboard and the two groups switch roles. When the A teams have finished, the first game is over.

3. Stop the games ten minutes before the period ends so that the class may discuss what it has learned and apply it to composition. Be sure the class recognizes the importance of saying something simply and precisely because it saves time and minimizes confusion. Point out that written equivalents to gestures are metaphors, images, examples, and precise descriptive words and that all are very useful in clarifying meaning.

Teaching Notes

• Competitive scoring generally appeals to students, but the exercise could be used merely as a demonstration, with no scoring at all.
• Be certain to leave time in the class period for the follow-up discussion. The purpose of the activity is to show the students the parallel between reconstructing a model through speech and reconstructing an image or idea through writing.

Variations

a. TinkerToys were selected for this exercise because they provide descriptive handles (shape, size, color) and because they are appropriate for three-dimensional structures that hang together well. Substitute tools like toothpicks or even pencils could be used, however; or the tools could be scrapped entirely in favor of a line drawing on paper. The object is to provide a reproducible figure to challenge communication skills.

b. For a demonstration of a more descriptive nature, use scenic pictures instead of TinkerToys. Divide the class into groups of four or five and give one person from each group a picture. Have that person describe the scene to the others in the group, who will individually draw what they think the speaker is seeing. The diverse papers produced will provide the basis for a discussion of effective methods of description and of the variety of responses readers bring to one writer's words.

27 Images

The study of poetic imagery demonstrates to students the writer's obligation to transmit a picture from his or her own mind to that of the reader. In an imaginative effort, students are first asked to take written images and create nonwritten translations of them. Then they are given nonwritten images and asked to translate those into words. The activity helps the students draw the parallel between literature and other art, and it enables them to express themselves through their individual interests and skills as well as through writing.

Objectives

- Students learn to recognize imagery.
- Students relate the printed word to alternative modes of expression.

Materials

- poetry containing vivid imagery that appeals to the age group (see Teaching Aid No. 30)
- art supplies
- tape recorders
- pictures and recordings

Teaching Sequence

1. Explain *imagery*. Read and discuss several poems that contain vivid, appealing images. Review *simile* and *metaphor*.
2. Discuss how artists other than poets and writers translate an image they see or feel in such a way that their audiences may also see or feel it. List as many types of artists as possible—painters, playwrights, dancers, mimes, architects, songwriters, composers, and so on.
3. Hand out more poetry and give the students time to read it and mark images which appeal to them personally. Then ask them to plan a translation of one of those images into another art form, such as a drawing, a piece of music, (original or not), a sound recording, an architectural design, an auto design, a textile work, a dance routine, or a mime.

"Birches," Robert Frost
"#15, A Coney Island of the Mind," Lawrence Ferlinghetti
"Dog," Lawrence Ferlinghetti
"Poppies in October," Sylvia Plath
"Morning Song," Sylvia Plath
"Ride a Wild Horse," Hannah Kahn
"Dover Beach," Matthew Arnold
"Chicago," Carl Sandburg
"Fog," Carl Sandburg
"Grass," Carl Sandburg
"Elegy for Jane," Theodore Roethke
"The Tiger," William Blake
"Intimations of Immortality" (excerpts), William Wordsworth
"Ode to the West Wind," Percy Bysshe Shelley

4. Allow the students class time to plan their translations. Try to work briefly with each student to be sure each one recognizes the images in the hand-out and understands the assignment. If students need school equipment, such as cassette recorders, cameras, or art supplies, help them check it out.

5. Set aside a class period for the presentations of the translated images. Have the students read their images before showing their translations and encourage discussion and questions about the work.

6. During another class period, run the assignment in reverse, providing a variety of visual or audio images for the students to record in words. Suggest that they first list words describing the impression the picture or sound made on them, then choose the most descriptive words, and build images around them. Present Frost's poem, "Birches", and examine the poet's vivid translations of the arched birches and the shattered ice: girls drying their hair and broken glass from the arc of the sky.

Teaching Notes

• Most of the students will translate the images with drawings, even those with distinct talents in other areas. Encourage the students to reach into themselves for an individual means of expression.

• Step 4 will of course depend somewhat on the media and art supplies available in the school. Many teenagers, however, have their own cassette recorders, cameras, and other equipment, so the plan is feasible even where school stock isn't adequate.

• Videotapes may also provide inspiration in step 6, if a machine is available.

• Evaluate both the translation and the written imagery on appropriateness and originality.

Variation

Rather than having the students read their images prior to showing their translations, let the student audience guess the image. Compile and duplicate a list of the specific images the class has chosen to translate. After each presentation, let the class pair the original image to its new art form.

28 Tourist Almanac

This almanac is an excellent group project that incorporates both writing and research skills. Students are assigned short, interesting articles that may be tailored to their interests and abilities. The research element acquaints them with their community's history and services, and the artwork option lets them demonstrate their nonliterary skills.

Objectives

• Students practice effective and interesting descriptive writing.
• Students do field work and utilize community resources.

Materials

• a sample tourist brochure or almanac

Teaching Sequence

1. Bring the tourist guide or almanac to class and read some sample entries aloud. Discuss the nature of the articles and their tendency to be dully repetitive in vocabulary and format. Point out their brevity and persuasiveness as well and note that their claims are sometimes exaggerated. Reread a short entry from the guide and call for suggestions for improving it.

2. Explain that the class is going to write a tourist almanac for their city. If the city is too small to justify such a venture, base the guide on a nearby larger city or on an imaginary one. List the services and attractions that would interest a tourist. Include articles on such subjects as the landmarks, climate, and native flora and fauna.

3. Keeping in mind the varied abilities and interests of the students, assign each the coverage of one feature or attraction of the city. Point out that human interest factors, brief historical backgrounds, and illustrations make an entry more appealing, and that trite summations or repetitive come-ons kill reader interest.

4. Help the students plan their research. Provide lists of places, such as the chamber of commerce, historical society, and city archives, where they may find information. Help them arrange interviews with long-time residents or business people and otherwise open investigative doors. Be sure they've prepared lists of questions and have an objective in mind before entering the field. Recommend that those with purely descriptive assignments visit the places before writing, even if ample research material is available.

5. Suggest that each student also submit at least one "filler," such as a joke, aphorism, or short item not worth a full article, to intersperse between the articles.

6. Allow photography or artwork to accompany the articles.

7. Post the results in the classroom for all to enjoy.

Teaching Notes

• Come to class the first day prepared with some historical facts about the city and with some lists of services and attractions. Not all the students will be aware of these facts or offerings.

• Warn the students to rely upon their writing, rather than their artwork, to convey their messages.

- Grade the articles on conciseness and appeal and allow extra credit for artwork.

Variations

a. Involve the graphic arts or business department in the project and print the almanac. Prepare for printing from the start by assigning a certain amount of space for each article. Warn students that illustrations must be kept small and be appropriate for the copying processes available.

b. Before assigning specific articles to the students, plan a tour of the city that will include as many as possible of its best attractions. Then write the tourist manual as a step-by-step tour guide.

c. If the subject city is too large for the inclusion of both attractions and services, narrow the scope to just the historical landmarks.

d. Combine the exercise with the study of Edgar Lee Masters' *Spoon River Anthology*. Have the tourist almanac entries written in verse, imitating the tone and style of Masters' epitaphs.

29 Mystery Biographies and Critiques

This writing exercise is easily integrated with literature studies as either a research exercise or a review game. Using facts about authors, works, trends, and eras, students write descriptive passages without actually naming their subjects. The mystery biographies and critiques they produce may then be used as an identification game for class review.

Objectives

- Students research topics and share their findings.
- Students practice recording facts clearly, logically, and interestingly.

Materials

- prepared list of subjects to cover
- numbered bibliography list and assignment cards
- literature texts and/or reference materials

Teaching Sequence

1. In advance of the lesson, make a numbered list of all the authors, works, and terms to be covered. Duplicate the list for distribution. Also prepare enough small cards for all students, writing on each card a number to correspond with an item on the list. Assignments may be designated for particular students at this stage, if desired.

2. Pass out the numbered list to the class and tell them they each will be writing a mystery biography, description, or critique of one of the items on the list. Explain that they should stress facts covered in class but may also research additional interesting material for their writings. They *must not name* the author, work, or term they are covering; they should instead stress the important contributions, the special characteristics, or the long-range influences on literature that make the entries noteworthy.

3. Set a due date and allow some class time for research.

4. On the due date, use the mystery writings for a classroom activity. Have the students take turns reading their descriptions aloud so the class, either individually or in teams, may identify their subjects.

Teaching Notes

• Exercise the option in step 1 for individualizing the assignments. Challenge brighter students with more difficult literary works or ideas to describe.

• Grade the writings on originality, thoroughness, and clarity.

Variations

a. Have students write pairs of descriptions, one favorable and one unfavorable, about their items. This approach will encourage them to use critical reviews in their research and to pin down their own responses to a work or a literary style. The writings may still be used for class review.

b. Let the students assume the identities of the authors or of the main characters in the works and have them write autobiographies. Apply step 4 to this variation.

c. If language arts and social studies are taught together, use the activity as a history, rather than a literary, review.

d. Conduct the review game as a silent seatwork assignment. Have the students pass the papers in a set pattern around the classroom at intervals cued by the teacher. Direct the students to record their answers by the number of the assignment and turn in the answer sheet when they have read all the descriptions. Be sure to have a number of writings prepared to cover incompletes, so that every student will have a paper during each time interval.

30 Bestiary

An imaginative activity with numerous possibilities for variation, the Bestiary is basically an assignment in sensory description. The entire class participates in creating a bestiary; each member contributes the description of one creature fitting a classification chosen by the group. The class should be familiar with sensory description before starting to write the bestiary.

Objectives

- Students practice writing sensory description.
- Students study a medieval art form.

Materials

- a bestiary or excerpts from one, preferably illustrated
- a sample bestiary entry (see Teaching Aid No. 31)

Teaching Sequence

1. Introduce the bestiary as a literary form. List and discuss its major characteristics—a religious basis, its use as a medical reference and a natural history, the inclusion of mythical beasts, and illustrations.
2. Read and display entries from a bestiary. Discuss at least one of the entries in detail, pointing out the elements discussed in step 1. Mention that the familiar unicorn appeared in nearly all early bestiaries as a mythical beast illustrating a religious embodiment, Christ and purity. Discuss how a bestiary may be moralistic without being specifically religious. (see Teaching Notes)
3. Briefly review sensory description.

4. Decide as a class what kind of bestiary to produce (see variations). Record on the board the types of information each entry must contain and note that students are free to include more. For example, list that the entry must describe the beast, draw some moral parallel between its behavior and human behavior, and enumerate the medical uses of its body (see Teaching Aid No. 31). Point out that the tone of the bestiary is quite serious, even when the beasts are mythical. As a group, develop a sample bestial description on the board.

5. Allow the students to illustrate their entries for extra credit but stress that writing is the point of the assignment. Set the due date.

6. Collect, correct, and post the papers.

Teaching Notes

• If the class is too old to enjoy hashing out a format together in step 4, present them with an established style to follow.

• The literary style of some early bestiaries is not worth imitating. Stress that the elements of good composition apply to the assignment.

• Stress that entries don't have to exemplify a religious principle, or eliminate the religious aspect altogether. A description can make a strong moral statement or behavioral parallel without being religious.

• Emphasize that the writing, not the artwork, is the point of the assignment.

• Encourage the students to stretch their imaginations and create fictional creatures unless the assignment is based upon true natural history.

• Grade the papers on the elements of sensory description in particular and of good composition in general. Include a consideration for adherence to the format chosen by the class and for creativity.

Variations

a. Specify that all the creatures must be fanciful—no actual or traditional mythical beasts allowed.

b. Specify that all the creatures must be real but that medicinal uses and the morals or parallels drawn from their behaviors are up to the fancy of the writer.

TEACHING AID NO. 31
Sample Bestiary Entries

Sample #1: Entry based upon Human Characteristics

The Zero

Great persistence and scholarship are required to recognize the zero, an unusual and self-effacing animal that inhabits most of the globe. The creature has no standard size or shape but ranges from a handful to an armful in bulk and from lanky to cuddly in form. Its fur is also not standard in color or texture.

The call of the zero is soft and melodic and usually doesn't rise above the sounds of its neighbors. Often other zeros do not even hear it, through they are, of course, more delicately attuned to it. The odor of a zero is similarly subtle because the creature is extremely fastidious.

The outstanding behavioral characteristic of the zero is its deep-seated reluctance to call attention to itself, even when its actions are meritorious. Preferring to establish its own pace and achieve its own often rigorous goals, it avoids imposing its standards upon others of its own or related species. As a result, it is a valuable but seldom noticed or rewarded citizen of the animal world.

When a zero is identified and domesticated, it is a true and loving pet; allowed to sleep with an infant, it will make the child a more perceptive and intelligent person. The zero is seldom tamed, however, because it is so difficult to recognize; therefore, naturalists believe, numerous zeros may still exist in the wild.

Sample #2: Entry Based upon a Real Animal

The Cat

The cat is a common but diabolical creature that some misguided persons keep as a pet. Full-grown, it is only about a foot tall and has a tantalizingly soft appearance; but its insides are filled with evil vapors from Satan's dwelling. Occasionally the animal will vent some of these gases from its mouth in fearful hissing or spitting; and whoever is touched by the fetid air is subsequently less able to resist the devil. The cat also has

Continued on next page.

spears sheathed in its paws and can fling them out at an attacker much the same as a porcupine can. These razor-sharp lances contain the same spiritual toxins as the cat's breath.

The cat is tolerated because it masquerades as a boon to the household by killing other Satanic creatures like the rat. However, smart observers know, the animal gets its real sustenance from the blood of infants. A stealthy killer, the cat will suck a sleeping babe's blood through the piercing, hollow fangs concealed under its furred upper lip. The spirit of the infant is then consigned to Satan forever.

When a cat dies, the evil spirit within it escapes with the animal's death howl. The carcass, however, is still vile and must be pitched into a roaring fire. No one should stand in the then contaminated smoke.

c. Direct the students to write about only one variety of creatures, such as birds, insects, mammals, or reptiles.

d. Expand the assignment to include the universe and the imagined inhabitants of real and fictitious planets.

e. Base the bestiary on human models and behaviors. Use satirical stereotypes found in a school, in national politics, in an occupation, or in an historical era. Do some samples in class to illustrate the idea.

CHAPTER 8 Take Off on the Greats

31 Fable

The fable, which is often included in literature studies, provides an attractive imitative writing assignment. It is short, has a definite format, and gives the students two chances for creative thinking: the development of a proverb and the embodiment of it. The fable also encourages them to study people's behavioral patterns in order to formulate a proverb.

Objectives

- Students practice writing within a structured format.
- Students create representative situations and consistent characters.

Materials

- fables for class analysis
- proverbs for discussion and inspiration (see Teaching Aid 32)
- dictionaries
- thesauri

Teaching Sequence

1. Read a number of fables from Aesop, choosing stories that vary in length and morals that vary in complexity. Point out that the genre
- is short
- uses creatures who behave like humans
- exemplifies a maxim which is stated at the end
- seldom has more than two characters
- may state a moral in terms borrowed from the story ("The Daw in Borrowed Plumes")
- may generalize a moral from the story ("The Lion and the Gnat")

Point out that a fable with a generalized moral is more interesting to read and more difficult to write. Such a fable requires the author to create a story which exemplifies a broad generality. The fable directly echoing the moral, on the other hand, is easier to write because both the characters and the situation are provided by the moral itself.

An exhaustive listing of proverbs is available in *Dictionary of American Proverbs*, ed. David Kin, Philosophical Library: New York, 1955.

1. A beard well lathered is half shaved.
2. All cats look gray in the dark.
3. Haste makes waste.
4. In spite of colleges and schools, the world remains a ship of fools.
5. Don't saw off the branch you're sitting on.
6. Don't put the carriage before the horse.
7. Who hangs on, wins.
8. Let sleeping dogs lie.
9. Don't buy a pig in a poke.
10. Pride goeth before a fall.
11. Everything comes to the one that can wait.
12. The sheep who talks peace with a wolf will soon be mutton.
13. The one who laughs last laughs best.
14. Look before you leap.

2. Hand out the sample proverbs and go over them. Spend a few moments letting students recall other proverbs or create some of their own. Add them to the list.

3. Choose one proverb from the list and, as a class, develop a fable around it. Choose and define characters and a simple story, recording the outline on the board.

4. Assign the composition of a fable based upon a proverb chosen from the list or created by the student. Stress again the basic elements of the genre and its essential simplicity.

5. Read aloud and post the most inventive fables.

Teaching Notes

• The exercise succeeds because it supplies the basic story materials to average students and challenges gifted ones to create independently.

• The Thurber fable, "The Owl Who Was God," could be read

along with the Aesop fables, especially if oral activities are part of the classroom program. This fable is delightful as a group reading and makes a very important statement about mob intellect. It is also an excellent example of creative interpretation of the genre. Other humorous uses of the form by James Thurber or Edward Lear could also be used to introduce a satirical fable as a follow-up.

• Keep dictionaries and thesauri handy. The language of Aesop's fables is archaic and imposing and will require discussion and definition. If the students are to imitate the style as well as the format, they will need thesauri to increase their vocabularies.

• Because of the difficult language in the fables, the lesson will begin better if each student has a copy of what is being read.

• In grading, stress simplicity, originality, and the mechanics of writing.

Variations

a. Older, or more capable, students may be encouraged to imitate the heavy, adjectival style of the originals, to supply their own proverbs, and to write specific stories for a generalized moral.

b. For extra credit, allow illustration of the fable. Illustrations from a fable collection would show how the artwork may be as simple as the story and still make the same point. Do not let the artwork take over as the object of the assignment.

c. Instead of reading all through the better papers, leave off the moral summations and let the class formulate their own. Compare the class's morals to the author's, and discuss how simply and directly the fable must be written to precipitate a common conclusion.

32 Picture Story

Picture Story is a relatively simple inspirational method that may be tailored to different age groups by varying the difficulty of the requirements. Basically, the instructor provides a variety of pictures and asks each student to select one and write a story based upon it. The activity encourages students to consider cause-and-effect relationships and hypothesize events and explanations. It is generally attractive to all the students because so many interests may be covered by the pictures. Students will need either previous experience with story writing or a good introduction to it before attempting the assignment.

Objectives

- Students seek a logical explanation for a situation.
- Students practice presenting ideas in a logical order.
- Students review story elements.

Materials

- a large number of mounted, or otherwise protected, pictures clipped from magazines that appeal to the age group
- an illustrated literature text

Teaching Sequence

1. Discuss the object of the activity. To demonstrate what may be inferred from a picture, examine the illustration(s) from an unfamiliar story in the literature text. Ask the students what the story might be about, judging by the picture(s). Then have them read the story to see how close they came. Note how many different explanations were inspired by the picture(s) and how all of them *could* have been correct.

2. Select a picture from the ones brought to class and, as a group, outline a story based upon it. Seek ideas that transcend the obvious and discover the implied information illustrated in the pictures.

3. Working with the same outline, review the elements of a short story. Write them on the board.

4. Give the students time to look through the pictures and select one that suggests to them a story. Set a time limit to keep them on target.

5. Allow time for the students to individually brainstorm ideas from their pictures. Circulate through the classroom and assist students who look uninspired. Possible questions to ask them include:

- What could have happened to make that person (animal, scene) look that way?

- What could all these people have in common to bring them together here? Is this a celebration, a commiseration, or an accidental gathering?
- What about that individual's lifestyle brought him or her to this situation? What will his or her reaction be?
- What just happened? Why?
- What is going to happen next?
- What may be going on unseen in this picture?
- What is that person thinking about? Why?
- Pretend you are that person and write about what you are doing there.

6. Set a due date and remind the students they must hand in the picture with the paper.

7. Read or post the stories that reveal good form and original, penetrating thought by their authors.

Teaching Notes

- Avoid bringing entire magazines to class. The printed matter will distract the students and, in some cases, prevent original thought about the pictures. Captions should be removed from the pictures as well.
- Have ample pictures, twice as many as are needed for the number of students, and include duplicate or similar ones.
- Be sure to include the widest possible range of interests when selecting the pictures.
- Many students will need assistance in transcending the trite and obvious about their pictures. Spend as much time as possible circulating and advising to be sure they are reaching for the deeper implications.
- Grade the papers on mechanics, story elements, and originality of thought.

Variations

a. Post the pictures and stories in a scattered arrangement and allow class members time to try to match up the stories and the pictures.

b. As an alternative or an advanced lesson, have each student select two or more pictures and write a story that relates them. Do a sample story as an explanation, and stress that well-stretched imaginations can link many scenes that appear unrelated at first glance.

33 Stories-in-the-Round

Writing stories-in-the-round demonstrates graphically how a story may take a turn many times during its creation and how characters may remain consistent regardless of events. In the activity, a story is begun by a student or group of students, then passed periodically to other students or groups, each of whom adds to the story until it is completed. Students are repeatedly challenged to analyze what has already occurred in order to make a realistic change or a consistent addition.

Objectives

- Students become more familiar with the elements of a story.
- Students practice logical development.
- Students practice character consistency.

Materials

- regular classroom supplies

Teaching Sequence

1. Review the elements and basic action of a short story by reading and analyzing one in class. Note how many chances an author has to turn the plot.
2. Explain the activity thoroughly.
3. If the activity is to be conducted in groups, divide the class into groups of no more than four students each. Students of similar ability should be placed together. Have each group appoint a scribe. Assign each group a number and have the scribe record it on their paper.
4. Tell the groups that each will start a story, establishing within a set amount of time the setting, characters, and initial action. Stress that no more than two individual characters may be included. Explain that at the end of the first time period they will pass the story to another group and receive some other group's story themselves. They will then further the action of the new story. The stories will be circulated several times.
5. Write on the board the work to be accomplished during each time period. Each period should cover a short story element:

#1 Establishment of time, place, characters, and initial incident

#2 Introduction of conflict

#3 Rising action

#4 Climax

#5 Dénouement

#6 Conclusion

6. Set the time limit and allow the groups to start writing. When the time is up, signal them to trade papers in a clockwise motion.

7. Before the groups begin writing again, remind them that they are only to further the action of the story they have received. They are *not* to bring in elements from the stories they themselves originated. Note that they can turn the events of a story as long as they make a logical, believable, consistent turn. Set a time limit and let them create the conflicts in the stories. Continue in the same manner until every story element has been written into the story and the story is considered completed.

8. Direct the scribes to return the stories to the groups that originated them. Allow a few moments for the students to enjoy their stories before collecting the papers.

9. Read the papers aloud for the class and compare them to the story analyzed at the beginning of the activity. Evaluate their characters, viewpoints, and plots.

Teaching Notes

• This activity requires at least two class periods to complete. Older or very capable classes could spend longer and work for greater depth in their stories.

• The class must have some previous experience with and understanding of the short story before this exercise is attempted.

• Group the students by similar ability so everyone will feel free to offer ideas. Heterogeneous grouping will result in domination by the brighter or more creative students.

• Stress the reminder in step 7. A group that brings the elements of its own story into all the others destroys them all.

• Don't expect the products to be publisher's delights. Base grading on the participation and originality observed while circulating and helping. The real object of the assignment is to develop story elements and polish writing techniques.

Variations

a. Conduct the activity as an individual assignment rather than a group effort. For each exchange, have the students pass their stories to other individuals in the class.

b. If the assignment accompanies an intensive unit on the short story, assign each group a certain type of story and have it note that type with the group number at the top of the paper it circulates. For example, different groups could start humorous or serious stories, or approach the stories in omniscient, limited omniscient, first person, or direct observer point of view. They may also incorporate different tenses and tones. Increasing the difficulty of the assignment in this manner must also mean increasing the amount of time devoted to it. Grading should include a group grade for the work done on each story.

c. Form groups. Prepare a story beginning (time, place, characters, and original action) and give the same beginning to each group. Have each group finish the story itself; don't have the papers rotated as in the original assignment. Encourage the students to brainstorm follow-up ideas and stretch for something unusual so all the stories will turn out differently. Give a group grade as well as individual grades for participation.

d. Assign bizarre stories, such as fantasy or science fiction, in which turns and twists may defy Earth logic.

34 Old News

Besides being an enjoyable writing assignment, Old News is easily integrated with a literature or history study program. Using a city paper as a model, students role play different types of reporters and imagine the newsworthy items encountered in an earlier period of history. Each student may experience both group cooperation and individual expression of a special interest; and creative students can stretch for the unusual without leaving the others behind.

Objectives

• Students become familiar with newspaper format.
• Students practice impartial tone and succinct writing.

- Students review material from literature or history class.
- Students manipulate the elements of a story.

Materials

- local or city newspapers

Teaching Sequence

1. Examine as a class the newspapers brought to class. Enumerate the different kinds of news they contain and define the different kinds of reporters who worked on them.

2. As a class, select and focus on an historic era and design a newspaper that would have met the interests of the people of that era. Name the paper, establish the format, and assign different reporting roles to the students. Allow the students to include artwork or photography but stress that the writing, not the illustration, is the object of the assignment. Keep a record of who is covering what story.

3. On a set day, "read" the newspaper by having individual students read their articles aloud in the order in which they would appear in the printed paper. Then, collect the articles for grading or have an appointed staff of production editors copy articles onto dittoes laid out as newspaper pages. Duplicate and distribute the pages.

Teaching Notes

- Be careful to keep the articles in a realistic proportion. There are always more news items in a paper than there are gossip and advice columns, feature stories, humorous columns, sports articles, or social events.
- Stress that artwork is an extra credit addition, not the main point of the assignment. The stories are to be told primarily with words.
- If a good product is to be rendered, some library or other research time must be allowed.
- When choosing an historical era, narrow it to a time span that can realistically be covered. The classical Greek era, for example, could be restricted to the time of the Battle of Marathon or the return from Troy. The long Elizabethan Age could be limited to a single event, such as the circumnavigation of the globe by Sir Francis Drake or the burning of the Globe Theater. (see Variations)

• Grade the papers for mechanics, accuracy of data, and originality of presentation.

Variations

a. For older students, base the paper on an era covered in a literary work such as a Shakespearean play, a Hemingway or Steinbeck novel or short story, or even a poem like Sandburg's "Chicago." Show the students how to ferret out happenings that appear as background, or even as action, in the text. For example, the Depression background in *Grapes of Wrath* can suggest articles on bank closings, mortgage foreclosures, mass emigration, economic predictions, or union movements. The events themselves, such as Tom's release from jail or his involvement in labor union activities, provide more personal, specific reports. Research time and guidance by the instructor are essential in this approach.

b. Allow each student to write a minipaper containing at least eight short, varied articles. Post the best papers.

c. Investigate school news and write a paper to be distributed in the school if the school has no regular paper.

d. Run the exercise strictly as a creative writing assignment which requires no researched data. Choose any date—past, present, or future—and let the students release their imaginations to invent news.

e. Incorporate this activity in a minicourse in journalism. Encourage accurate reporting as well as adherence to journalistic style in the articles and grade papers accordingly. This approach requires a great deal of time and does not fit into most composition programs.

35 Paraphrasing Literature

This is an activity that not only helps students restate an idea, but will help an entire class better understand a literary masterpiece. The students are given specific passages from the masterpiece to rewrite in their own words. In order to do so, they must analyze what they have read, sort out the ideas, and present them again in their own style—a process which reveals to them the universal and timeless qualities of good literature.

Hamlet, I, i, 23 – 28

Original Text
*Horatio says 'tis but our fantasy
And will not let belief take hold of him
Touching this dreaded sight, twice seen of us;
Therefore I have entreated him along
With us to watch the minutes of this night,
That if again this apparition come,
He may approve our eyes and speak to it.*

Paraphrased Text 1
Horatio says we're imagining this awful thing and won't believe we've seen it twice. So, I've asked him to accompany us on watch tonight, so if the ghost appears, he will believe us and talk to it.

Paraphrased Text 2
Hey, man, that Horatio dude don't believe we've seen this here ghost two times; he things we're on a trip. Well, I says to him, you stay up with us tonight, an' if the ghost comes, you take him on.

"Barn Burning," Faulkner

Original Text
Then he was moving, running, outside the house, toward the stable; this the old habit, the old blood which he had not been permitted to choose for himself, which had been bequeathed him willy nilly and which he had run for so long (and who knew where, battening on what of outrage and savagery and lust) before it came to him. *I could keep on*, he thought. *I could run on and on and never look back, never need to see his face again. Only I can't. I can't*, the rusted can in his hand now, the liquid sploshing in it as he ran back to the house and into it, into the sound of his mother's weeping in the next room, and handed the can to his father.

Continued on next page.

The assignment also holds many possibilities for additional challenges to gifted students.

Objectives

- Students analyze literature for individual word meaning.
- Students restate ideas in a logical, sensible way.
- Students learn paraphrasing, a skill they will use in research writing.

Materials

- a long literary selection divided into individual paraphrasing assignments tailored to the ability of every member of the class
- dictionaries

Teaching Sequence

1. Read and discuss the literature. It is essential that the students understand the material before they try to rewrite it.
2. Define *paraphrasing*. Take a passage from the work under current study and rewrite it (see Teaching Aid No. 33). Recommend that the students record the following procedure for their own use:
- Look up all the words you don't understand, and write in definitions for them.
- Make a list of all the ideas you must maintain in your own version.
- Rewrite the ideas, using your own words and referring to the definitions for ideas on how to simplify the vocabulary.
- Proofread and compare your passage to the original to make sure both say essentially the same thing.

3. Pass out the prepared assignments and provide class time to start working. Circulate and assist where necessary.

4. When the papers are due, collect and correct them. Return them to the class and reconstruct the original work by having the students read their paraphrases in the proper order. Discuss whether the modernized or simplified language changes the truth of the story. Point out the universality and timelessness of good literature that allow it to transcend differences in vocabulary and syntax. Discuss also the superior beauty, balance, meter, and descriptive power of the original.

Teaching Notes

• Plan the individual assignments carefully, giving the more difficult passages to the more capable students. Choose passages from the entire text so the whole story, play, or poem is represented by the selections. Include famous passages.

• Determine the number of lines per student by the amount of time the class will be devoting to the project.

• Some students will need a lot of help locating the ideas to list for restatement. Be sure to spend time circulating among these students.

• Grade on accuracy of translation and originality of language.

Variations

a. Restating material in simple terms will be very easy for some students. Try challenging these people to restate the passage in verse, even if the original work is prose.

b. If the original work is drama, let the class act it out through their paraphrases. Discuss how a modern setting, costume, and vocabulary still do not affect the humanistic premise of the work.

c. If the class is not to reconstruct the masterpiece as a whole from their passages, allow them to select their own lines to paraphrase. A possible set of guidelines would be:

• Working as an individual, paraphrase 40 consecutive lines. If the work is drama, include two or more speakers.

• As above, including a soliloquy if the work is drama.

• Working as a group, paraphrase several pages, allowing each member to do about 40 lines. If the work is drama, try to complete an entire scene.

36 Speech Pattern Comparisons

This enjoyable discussion and imitation activity has a dual purpose. On one level, students study the literary craft of differentiating characters by manipulating their speech habits. On another, they apply what they've learned about the subconscious impact of speech patterns to the types of speech they hear daily. In addition, they utilize TV time to reinforce classroom learning.

Objectives

• Students do an in-depth study of literary dialogue.
• Students analyze how their speech affects the image they project.
• Students relate media models to literature and composition.

Materials

• dialogue selections from established authors, copied for every student or recorded as a dramatic reading (see Teaching Aid No. 34)
• tape recordings of newscasts, game shows, children's shows, and popular programs
• cassette recorders (optional)

Teaching Sequence

1. Play back or read as many literary selections as possible that show intentional speech differentiation. Guide the students in analyzing the image each character projects through speech— level of self-confidence, level of education, type of work, intelligence, honesty, and superficiality or depth. Analyze individual speeches for the characteristics that create an impression about the speaker—vocabulary, slang, idiomatic expressions, correctness of grammar, length of sentences, calmness and consistency of logic, references to self or to interests, and allusions to others. (see Teaching Aid 34)

2. Discuss standard, colloquial, and substandard speech, using examples from the selections presented in step 1.

3. Discuss the stereotypes or anticipated speech of such individuals as English-speaking foreigners, teachers, judges,

TEACHING AID NO. 34

Sample Dramatic Dialogues

a. Huck, Jim, and Tom in *Huckleberry Finn*, Twain
b. Mack and Doc in *Cannery Row*, Steinbeck
c. The Judge, Mr. Harris, and Abner Snopes in "Barn Burning," Faulkner
d. The man and woman in "Hills Like White Elephants," Hemingway
e. Bottom and any of the lovers in *A Midsummer Night's Dream*, Shakespeare
f. to exemplify no artistic differences, any simple romance or mystery story

Sample Discussion:
Mack and Doc, **Cannery Row**, Chapter 9

Characteristics:

Doc	Mack
good grammar	poor grammar
complete sentences	incomplete sentences
reasonable tone	childish, wheedling tone
careful, reserved statements	heavy, repetitious use of slang
succinct explanations	crude language and cursing
	lack of forethought in speeches

Images:

smart, wary, educated, considerate, thoughtful, deep, sophisticated	thoughtless, hasty, careless, bohemian, shallow, poorly educated

ministers, children, blue-collar workers, office personnel, and others typically found in the students' environment. Draw examples from popular TV shows. Help the students pose explanations for these patterns.

4. For homework, assign the analysis of at least three different styles of speech. Suggest the students listen to friends, newscasters, various adults, radio announcers, or the characters on a TV show other than those used in the introductory

discussion. Specify that the analyses should follow the points outlined in the class discussion in step 1.

5. Use the analyses for a follow-up discussion during the next class before introducing the writing assignment.

6. Review the punctuation rules for dialogue. Assign the composition of a dialogue involving two or three characters only. Steer the better students away from reliance upon the obvious, overused styles like the southern accent or "street talk" (see Teaching Aid No. 35.)

7. Share with the class the dialogues that demonstrate clear characterization. Allow the authors of these to choose readers for an oral presentation.

Teaching Notes

• The assignment is challenging, so grading should be lenient. Slow and even average students will have difficulty avoiding the styles mentioned in step 6, but there is value in any imitation that reflects an understanding of speech differentiation and reveals an honest attempt at it.

• Point out to the students the differences that exist even between individuals of the same profession, for example between two teachers on the school staff, between Howard Cosell and Don Meredith, or between Jessica Savitch and Barbara Walters.

• Tell the students to avoid TV commercials in their analyses. Commercials, as a rule, simplify language and overdo visual stereotyping and are not realistic examples of speech. They might be used as an exaggerated example in step 1.

• In pursuing the discussion in step 2, take care to keep the comments analytical, not critical. The purpose is not to ridicule any style of speech or to create social stratification. Discuss the destructive potential of stereotyping.

• The selections for step 1 are most effective if presented as a dramatic reading on tape, with printed copies for the students to follow and to use during the discussion. A variety of voices, rather than just the teacher's own, also increases the effectiveness of the taped readings.

Variations

a. For the speech analyses, allow students to tape real conversations or dialogues from the media and do oral, rather than written, analyses. Stress the inclusion of distinctly different styles of life and speech.

b. Have the students tape or otherwise preserve actual conversations with the same number of participants as are included in one of the literary samples studied in class. Then have them rewrite the taped conversation in the styles of the speakers in the literature.

c. Instead of having each student produce a written dialogue, divide the class into groups of four students of mixed ability. Have each group produce a dialogue between two characters. Each character's lines should be written by a pair of the students. The teacher should assist each group with the work.

d. Instead of requiring whole dialogues of the students, present them with a number of sentences in simple, standard English and ask them to rewrite each sentence in two different speech styles. Possible styles could be those of:

- a child of six
- an uneducated laborer (farmer, trapper, coal worker, domestic employee, fruit picker, or the like)
- a person conversant in popular slang
- a very educated person (judge, doctor, professor, minister, or the like)
- a very old person

e. Use this lesson to lead into activity 25, Dramatic Dialogues.